101
Ways to Power Up
Your Job Search

J. Thomas Buck

William R. Matthews

Robert N. Leech

McGraw-Hill

New York   San Francisco   Washington, D.C.   Auckland   Bogotá
Caracas   Lisbon   London   Madrid   Mexico City   Milan
Montreal   New Delhi   San Juan   Singapore
Sydney   Tokyo   Toronto

Library of Congress Cataloging-in-Publication Data

Buck, J. Thomas (John Thomas).
    101 ways to power up your job search / J. Thomas Buck, William R.
Matthews, Robert N. Leech.
        p.   cm.
    Includes index.
    ISBN 0-07-041043-7 (pbk.)
    1. Job hunting.   I. Matthews, William R. (William Robert).
II. Leech, Robert N.   III. Title.
HF5381.B679   1997
650.14—dc21
                                                        96-51986
                                                            CIP

McGraw-Hill

A Division of The McGraw·Hill Companies

1   2   3   4   5   6   7   8   9   0   DOC/DOC   9   0   2   1   0   9   8   7

ISBN 0-07-041043-7

*The sponsoring editor for this book was Betsy Brown, the editing supervi-
sor was Fred Dahl, and the production supervisor was Claire Stanley. It was
set in Frugal Sans by Inkwell Publishing Services.*

Printed and bound by R. R. Donnelley & Sons Company

McGraw-Hill books are available at special quantity discounts to use as pre-
miums and sales promotions, or for use in corporate training programs. For
more information, please write to the Director of Special Sales, McGraw-Hill,
11 West 19th Street, New York, NY 10011. Or contact your local bookstore.

 This book is printed on recycled, acid-free paper containing a minimum of 50% recycled, de-inked fiber.

Contents

List of Tools   v

Foreword   vii

Introduction   xi

Acknowledgments   xv

I. DEFINING YOURSELF

Chapter 1. Getting Off to a Good Start: Letting Your Values and Feelings Be Your Career Guide   3

Chapter 2. Avoiding Traps and Controlling Your Job Search Direction   13

Chapter 3. Leveraging Accomplishments   23

Chapter 4. Know Thyself, Sell Thyself   35

II. TARGETING YOUR MARKET

Chapter 5. Choosing Your Job Instead of Letting It Choose You   59

Chapter 6. The Best Companies to Work For: Creating Your Personal List   77

Chapter 7. Everything You've Always Wanted to Know about Potential Employers .. but Didn't Know Who or What to Ask   95

Chapter 8. The Point of No Return: What to Do Before Setting Forth on the Interview Path   105

III. SECURING YOUR POSITION

Chapter 9. How to Build Your Own Network from Scratch   115

Chapter 10. Reworking Resumes   129

Chapter 11. Become Your Own Telemarketer   141

Chapter 12. The Interview: Preparing Yourself to Be Grilled and
Coming Out Well-Done   149

Chapter 13. How Did the Interview Go?   165

Chapter 14. Responding to the Offer .. or the Lack of One   183

Chapter 15. Stepping Back, Moving Forward   197

Chapter 16. Your Career Search Doesn't End with Your Next Job   207

Index   219

Strategic Career Search Model & Outline

Power Up! Your Job Search

List of Tools

1. Where Do You Need Career Help?   xiii
2. Values Reality Check   4
3. Know Your Spiral   7
4. Express Yourself   9
5. Find Your Sticking Points   10
6. Getting Unstuck   11
7. Look for Your Blind Spot   11
8. Try to Find Your Personal Career Trap   14
9. State Your Preferences   16
10. Choose Your Ideal Working Environment   18
11. Word Association   19
12. Choose Your Organizational Culture   20
13. Finding Your Job Comfort Zone   21
14. Lifeline   24
15. Quick Quiz—The Weirdest Job Interview You'll Never Have   26
16. Significant Experiences   28
17. Alien Encounter   29
18. Things to Do with Accomplishments   31
19. Turning Accomplishments into Skills   33
20. Skill Selecting   36
21. Attributes: A to Z   37
22. Working with Style: Which One Fits You?   40
23. Find the Strengths in Your Style   45

24. Translating Your Style into Work Behaviors   47
25. Choose Your Power Words   49
26. Seeing Yourself through Others' Eyes   52
27. So You Wanna Be a ...   55
28. Multiple Choice—Test What's Really Important to You   60
29. Wanted: The Perfect Job   63
30. From Fantasy to Reality   65
31. Worst-Case Scenarios   67
32. Magnet Skill   69
33. Draw Your Own Conclusions   70
34. Refining Your Choices   72
35. The Match Game   74
36. Your Surprise Package   76
37. Back to the Want Ads   78
38. Brainstorming Information Sources   79
39. Organization/Job Type Matching   82
40. Multiply the Possibilities   86
41. Draw on Your Industry Knowledge   89
42. Industrial Espionage   93
43. Are These Organizations Right for You?   96
44. Scavenger Hunt   97
45. The Ten Worst List   99
46. The Ten Best List   100
47. Finding Information Nuggets   101

48. Skill Comparison Analysis   *106*

49. Listening to the Gossip   *107*

50. Inside Stuff   *109*

51. I Will Not Be Tempted By...   *111*

52. What's Your NIQ (Networking Instinct Quotient)?   *116*

53. Identifying Your Natural Network   *119*

54. Target Networking   *120*

55. Find the Shared Trait   *122*

56. Mix Your Networks   *124*

57. Target Shifting   *125*

58. Create Your Own Rumor   *127*

59. Getting the Word Out!   *128*

60. Grade Your Resume   *130*

61. Fun Things to Do with Resumes   *131*

62. Two Resumes for the Price of One   *133*

63. Putting Your Best Piece of Paper Forward—Type of Organization   *136*

64. Putting Your Best Piece of Paper Forward—Role of Interviewer   *137*

65. Cut Through the Clutter   *138*

66. What's Your PDQ (Phone Dialogue Quotient)?   *142*

67. The Perfect Comeback Line   *144*

68. Favorable Odds   *145*

69. Activate Your Pitch   *147*

70. The 12 Things to Do When You're Asking for an Interview   *148*

71. If All Else Fails—Last Resort Tactics   *150*

72. Making the Grade on the Job   *152*

73. 25 Questions Interviewers Frequently Ask   *153*

74. Knowing Your Interviewer   *156*

75. Extra Credit Questions   *160*

76. Interviewing with Style   *162*

77. Knowledge Is Power   *163*

78. Instant Replay: Keeping a What/How "Tape" of the Action   *166*

79. Self-Analysis   *170*

80. Turn Back the Clock   *173*

81. Know Thy Employer   *174*

82. The Interviewee Report Card   *176*

83. What's Wrong with This Interview?   *177*

84. Post-Interview Puzzlers   *184*

85. Magic Formula   *186*

86. Seven Questions to Ask Before Accepting Any Offer   *190*

87. Negotiating by the Numbers   *191*

88. If You Still Can't Decide   *192*

89. Rebounding from Rejection   *193*

90. Turning Rejection into Acceptance   *195*

91. Scan   *198*

92. 20-20 Hindsight   *200*

93. Define   *201*

94. Resolve   *203*

95. Implement   *204*

96. Are You a New or Old Paradigm Type of Person?   *209*

97. Acquiring Skills   *211*

98. What You Don't Know about Your Targeted Skills Can Hurt You   *213*

99. Individual Development Planning   *215*

100. Giving Back   *216*

101. Work Your Way to the Top   *217*

Foreword

101 Ways to Power Up Your Job Search fits the model for a paper-based performance support system. In fact, once it gets loaded onto the Internet with some HTML capabilities, it most likely will be the bible for job seekers. It provides just what you need, just when you need it, in just the right amount.

For seasoned professionals who have been through downsizing and workforce reductions, it is a great tool to renew and reinforce what you learned in the past but may have forgotten to maintain in the present. For new job seekers, it is a tool to help you identify who you are, what you work for, what you have to give, how to search for positions that have what you want, and so on.

Whether you're currently employed, just graduating, or between jobs, this book walks you through a step-by-step process that deals with your mental health and job security concerns. With downsizing, rightsizing, cost reduction, and early retirement hitting us from all sides, who isn't a little security conscious these days?

In today's chaotic business environment, individuals will be successful if they can focus both on what the business needs from them, as well as on what satisfaction they get from working. Those who gripe and growl about how bad it is, and how good it used to be, will be pushed to the side. This workbook provides you with the opportunity to proactively analyze your own needs and a business's needs to determine if there is a fit between the two. If not, it provides you the opportunity to seek for a better fit elsewhere. By working these applications, you can make the choice to go or stay before the situation stresses you out, or your performance puts you out.

You'll build confidence in your current competence, feel more secure with your capabilities, open avenues of employability you never knew existed, as well as build a network that will serve you throughout your career.

"You, Inc." will become a reality as you work through the activities. You'll begin to think of yourself and your capabilities from a sales perspective: "What value do I have to offer? How can I help this company? Where can I best apply my skills to support the achievement of this company's objectives?" And so on.

The book does not focus just on job seekers, but on those who are feeling disconnected and want to find a way to "fall back in love" with their current jobs. As organizations change, jobs change. Your challenge is to be prepared to know yourself and the company well enough to make good decisions about how you can best meet both the company's and your personal needs. Don't get caught in a job you can't stand: Prepare for the inevitable changes the future brings.

If you do not have self-confidence in your own competence, it is hard for those who work with you to have confidence and trust in your competence. This workbook helps you to gain (or regain) your self-confidence and self-trust. This new found (or rediscovered) confidence can then be applied to any position you wish: your current one or a new one. It's up to you to decide if your current job meets your needs, or if you desire to look outside and identify a job that better matches your competencies and work needs.

From the photographic map that guides the reader through the sections and chapters of the book, to the worksheets and work aids that clarify and simplify the work to be accomplished, this book is a keeper. You may not use it today, but you will use it sometime in the future. Maybe you picked it up to explore just who you are or to refresh your networking skills, or possibly to research another company. Whatever the reason, this is a book to purchase and keep on the shelf, because it is not a question of *if* you will use it, but of *when* you will need it.

I particularly like the Job-Finding Traps. How true! In my career counseling work with college graduates, I often encounter comments, thought processes, and barriers that parallel almost all the issues identified in this list.

Critical to future success and happiness with a job is the matching process between your personal needs and the job requirements. If you can't meet your personal needs through your job, there is little likelihood of success. If you're lucky, the mismatch will create such tension that you will become a voluntary turnover candidate, or be reduced by the company before the psycho-somatic illnesses begin to appear. If not, "Hello, pills and doctors."

The recommendation to manage your personal performance and record it on a monthly and yearly basis (in Chapter 3) is a wise idea. Your boss will be appreciative and you will be amazed at how much you get done. Measurement maximizes motivation; so you be the measurer of your own performance and tell the boss how you're doing.

I like the variety of ways Chapter 3 provides for identifying what is important to you in a job. Each of us gets different things from our jobs: Some of us like the money, some the accolades, some the friendships, and some the learning. What do you work for? Once you know *it,* you can share *it,* but the tough part is identifying *it* in the first place.

The matching of "What Is in It for You" and "What Is in It for the Company" to hire you, is the balanced perspective that all job seekers should assume. You must position yourself and your strengths to align with the company's needs. But never kid your-self and think you can get away with only considering the com-pany's side of the equation: Your side is just as important and has to be balanced with the company's.

The information on people networking provides a good un-derstanding of what a numbers game it is. The more contacts you make, the more likely you will find a job that matches your skills and desires. The fewer contacts you make, the less likely you will ever get the job you want. Unfortunately, it's also true that the more contacts you make, the more rejects you will experience. Maintaining a positive attitude, through the use of positive self-talk and good friends, is a must to be successful at the numbers game. Be prepared to share.

Another great assist is the recommendation to think twice and practice a bit before any interview. "Winging it" is for the birds—and a high-percentage risk when you only have one chance to make an impression on an interviewer. Remember, a bird in the hand *is* better than two in the bush.

I liked the "other-oriented" interview perspective recom-mended in the book. To see yourself as others see you is to feel secure with your knowledge of the company, the person, and the situation. This requires much research and preparation, but guarantees positive outcomes—maybe not every time, but there will always be a next time when you positively impress the interviewer.

Videotape yourself in an interview. I did. "Wow!!" What a learning process! I had a professional interviewer grill me with every question in the book. Only I saw the resulting video and learned from it. After I reviewed the video, the needs for change were obvious and most were easy to correct.

In the interviewing section, a thorough and complete list of questions to ask and prepare for during the interview is provided. Although many nonprofessional interviewers have their "pet" questions that require spontaneity and on-the-spot thinking, you will find that many of their odd questions have very little to do with the job. Try to tailor your answers so that your job-related strengths are highlighted.

A section to take note of is Negotiation. Frequently, job seekers are so excited that somebody wants them that they ignore the parameters of the offer and just take what they get. Be prepared with your list of musts and wants; otherwise you may not get any of them filled and regret it later.

The book ends with an emphasis on the future and the continuous improvement that all of us should be striving to achieve. Seeking and maintaining jobs is a never-ending process, and consists of many skill bases that can be continuously improved. Fortunately, these same skills are transferable to other applications and aren't unique to just job maintenance and hunting. In the chaotic business environment which most of us work, organizations occasionally outgrow the people who work for them; these people need this book to remind them how to locate a new job. More likely, you are continuously improving your skills and will outgrow your current job, thus creating the desire to move up or move on. This book is for you too.

Learn the skills this book offers and begin to apply them in all aspects of your personal, civic, academic, physical, work, and family life. They work!

CHAD COOK
Director—HRD, Rubbermaid

Introduction

The 101 exercises, games, and other tools that you'll find in the following pages can be used in different ways. Some of you will find them helpful in making difficult career choices. Others will try out the ones that seem like fun or pose an intellectual challenge. Still others will be intrigued by the tools that help you identify your specific career search strengths and weaknesses.

All this is fine, and we have no intention of dictating how you use this book. We should point out, however, that these 101 tools were not dropped randomly onto these pages. They are part of a strategic career search framework we've developed over the years. Originally, we designed a workbook as an alternative resource for people going through the outplacement process. The idea was to create a more user-friendly career search tool, one with a linked series of checklists, quizzes, and other exercises. Not only was this workbook highly accessible, but it provided a step-by-step strategy for a job or career search. We received so much positive feedback about the workbook, we decided to expand it into the book you're now reading.

The strategic framework is still in place, though we've added quite a bit of material for a more general readership (than our original audience of people going through outplacement). The book's three sections, the chapters within, and the exercises in the chapters are arranged purposefully. As a result, you may want to start at the beginning and work your way through. Take a look at the model at the end of the table of contents (page iv). The Strategic Career Search Model will help direct you to the sections that best fit your particular needs. Just open the book and start in the middle if that is where you want to get started or where your search is currently. The tools will still work for you, though in a more tactical way. It may be that you just need a catalyst to get yourself phoning for interview appointments. Or you could find yourself with a job offer, and you want to put it through the gauntlet of some of our exercises. A list of all 101 exercises is provided on pages v–vi. In fact, we assume that some people will just try one or two of the exercises because they've tried everything else—they're in the career doldrums, and they need a fresh idea for a job search or a new way of thinking about their careers.

Whatever your goal, we should confess that two biases are evident in our design of the 101 activities in this book. Those biases have to do with meaningful work and rapid change. In terms of the former, it is our conviction that we should seek work that helps us achieve meaning, that it isn't enough to seek jobs and careers only for financial rewards. As a result, some of our 101 tools help you discover what's really important in your life and in your work—the values and beliefs that a job might hold for you.

We've also designed our exercises in acknowledgment of how quickly jobs, careers, and industries are changing. Reengineering, rightsizing, and other trends make job tenure shorter than ever before. Similarly, people are taking more control of their working lives and changing jobs and careers more often than ever before. Second and even third careers are becoming increasingly common; people are also leaving large organizations to work for smaller ones or start their own businesses. Given all this, many of the exercises enable you to consider what changes you might want to make in your career or next job.

We recognize that some exercises will be more relevant to you than others. The situation for someone who has a job (but is unhappy with it) is different from that for someone who is out of work. It's also different for someone who is changing jobs versus someone who is changing careers. As much as possible, however, we've tried to create exercises that are applicable to all situations. We think you'll find a great deal of useful information here, packaged in an "interactive" way—to discover the information, you have to fill in a blank, choose the correct answer, role play, solve a puzzle. Not only will this provide you access to valuable information about the job marketplace and career search techniques, but it will help you learn more about the jobs and careers that best meet your particular needs. The first exercise—"Where Do You Need Career Help?"—will help you use this book effectively.

1. WHERE DO YOU NEED CAREER HELP?

Where Do You Need Career Help?								

Circle the number most representative of your satisfaction with the statement in the left-hand column. A (1) indicates no satisfaction and a (7) indicates you are very satisfied.

		Not Satisfied		Somewhat Satisfied			Very Satisfied	
1/2.	I have a good handle on my values with respect to work and potential jobs.	1	2	3	4	5	6	7
3/4.	I have deeply analyzed my skills and qualifications.	1	2	3	4	5	6	7
5.	I am very familiar with the potential jobs that would fit me.	1	2	3	4	5	6	7
6.	I have identified numerous organizations with the jobs that fit me.	1	2	3	4	5	6	7
7.	I have analyzed the types of organizations that I would most like to have a career in and that best match my values.	1	2	3	4	5	6	7
8.	I have focused my search on a specific list of potential employers that have jobs I qualify for and that I have a values match with.	1	2	3	4	5	6	7
9/10.	I am very comfortable with my awareness of networking strategies and tactics.	1	2	3	4	5	6	7
11/12.	I am very comfortable with my interviewing skills and ability to make a good impression.	1	2	3	4	5	6	7
13.	I perform a structured assessment of my interview performance following each interview opportunity.	1	2	3	4	5	6	7
14.	I have a structured approach to assess any offers I receive to ensure the best fit for my needs.	1	2	3	4	5	6	7
15.	I am very good at reviewing my total career search process to learn more effective approaches for my next move.	1	2	3	4	5	6	7
16.	I have identified my long-term career goals and have a plan for how to accomplish them.	1	2	3	4	5	6	7

Review your responses to these questions. Each item relates to a chapter in this book. If your satisfaction with particular items is low, you may want to concentrate your efforts in those chapters. If you are highly satisfied with some items, the book will help you fortify your strengths and your satisfaction.

This is unlike any career book you've ever read. It doesn't offer a theory about careers or focus on resume writing. More than anything else, it's designed to be usable, challenging, and fun. Some exercises will stretch you, encouraging out-of-the-box thinking that will help you view a job opportunity in new ways. Others use humor to help you discover useful facts about the world of work. You'll find lists, puzzles, maps, writing assignments, quizzes, games, and a variety of other tools in the following pages. We've tried to make the 101 activities as creative and innovative as possible—you've probably done all the boring career exercises already.

We come to this book with a different perspective from most authors. Prism Performance Systems isn't a search firm; our main business is helping individuals and organizations take charge of change—by designing change, by encouraging change, by training or learning in change, and by reacting to change constructively. Prism provides results-focused consulting on change projects, designs training and learning processes, designs and builds team-based organizations, and facilitates strategic planning and learning processes. Over the years, we've learned a great deal about job search issues because of our involvement with people processes; we've worked closely with human resources people on training and development issues and seen the career problems that confront people on the job. All this knowledge dovetails with our ability to create learning tools—we're constantly called upon to produce all types of exercises and games to help teams and individuals acquire new skills.

If it weren't for this unusual background, we couldn't create the 101 activities you'll find in the following pages. Though some of you might turn to them because you're having a dreary career day, we hope you'll also use them at other times—when you receive a new job offer, when you're thinking about a career change, when you're curious about what another job might be like. At the very least, we're sure they'll provide you with a new way of thinking about what you do for a living and why you do it.

Acknowledgments

Mark Twain once wrote, "What is there that confers the noblest delight? What is that which swells a man's breast with pride above that which any other experience can bring to him? Discovery! To know that you are walking where none others have walked; that you are beholding what human eye has not seen before; that you are breathing virgin atmosphere."[1] For us, writing our first book was a discovery process that brought all that and much more. But books never take shape through the work of the authors alone. The process involves a multitude of contributors deserving thanks.

Several coincidences came together to motivate the creation of *101 Ways to Power Up Your Job Search.* First was our interest at Prism in simulations, games, and exercises to facilitate performance and activate learning. Second was Bob's prior work on interviewing, resume writing, and job clubs. Next there was this constant churning we saw of people moving from job to job in many of our client organizations, in our communities, and in the many publications we read. Finally, there was the great feeling of dissatisfaction we sensed from so many people unhappy in their workplaces and the resulting "cost" to their families and their communities.

Thankfully, that constant churning and sense of dissatisfaction led one of our major clients to request that we create a workshop for their employees as the company completed a major reengineering effort. Their concern for their employees' welfare produced the seeds that grew into this book.

Our effort developing this book was very satisfying—the challenge of creating new approaches to difficult topics, the thinking it

[1]*The Columbia Dictionary of Quotations* is licensed from Columbia University Press. Copyright © 1993 by Columbia University Press. All rights reserved.

took to create a holistic model for job searching, the immediate, positive response from colleagues, and the fun of teaming together to develop the work. Our second acknowledgment therefore is to our creative team: Bill, Bob, Tom, and Bruce Wexler, who was integral in the creation of *101 Ways to Power Up Your Job Search*. We'd also like to thank Betsy Brown, our editor at McGraw-Hill, for her patience and guidance.

We would like to recognize the incredible support provided by the Prism team—our peer consultants/facilitators and our supporting marketing and finance teams. Special thanks goes to Prism's Publishing Group—Elizabeth Smith, Kim Olling, Lynn McRobb, and Carol Hubert, who did the typing and initial layout of the book, and willingly handled the many revisions and versions required to get a book ready for publication. Thanks, Team, for your help!

Additional thanks go to our other colleagues and our families who shape our ideas, and more importantly our values, on a daily basis in ways we rarely realize. Thanks to all!

Ultimately, this work has to be dedicated to all job searchers, with our hope and belief that you can find satisfaction and happiness in your jobs and careers. We hope your success will lead to the same happiness that we have achieved: with personal esteem, with your family, and in your community. Thanks for investing in our book, and best of luck.

1

DEFINING YOURSELF

1

Getting Off to a Good Start: Letting Your Values and Feelings Be Your Career Guide

Introduction

Some of you are looking for new jobs because you've been down-sized out of your old ones. Others still have jobs but are dissatisfied with them for any number of reasons—boredom, lack of recognition or responsibility, bad bosses, and so on. Some of you may be recent graduates looking for your first job. Whatever your situation, it's reasonable to expect that you're anxious, angry, or even depressed.

We've found that it's difficult for most people to begin job searches objectively and strategically. The emotions and attitudes fostered by an unhappy job situation (not to mention the financial factors for those out of work) make it all too easy to start out on the wrong foot.

To prevent that from happening, use the exercises and games in this chapter. You'll find a neat little exercise that will enable you to clarify what's really important to you in a job—it's amazing how often we're not conscious of what really matters until someone asks us.

Before we get to that exercise, however, we'd like to give you a chance to test your values.

2. VALUES REALITY CHECK

People tend to be unhappy and unsuccessful in jobs that are at odds with their personal values. Do you know what your values are? Have you ever considered whether a given job allows you to maintain those values? The following nine steps will allow you to run a reality check on your values. Given what you believe in, is it possible to find a job and an employer that match those values?

Step 1: Review this list of values. If there are two or three additional values that you feel should be on the list, add them.

Step 2: Using a pencil, rank each value in order of importance to you in the column marked, "Initial Rank." Do this step instinctively—don't spend a lot of time thinking about each value.

Step 3: Assume your work situation forces you to give up five of your values. Review your list and draw a line through the five you're willing to give up. As you draw the line, number each crossed-out value.

Step 4: Think about why you crossed off the five values. Ask yourself if it was your decision or if you were swayed by what others (family, friends, coworkers, society) believe. Change the values you crossed out and substitute others if, upon reflection, you decide your decision was influenced by others.

Step 5: Review your remaining ten values. Feel free to change your rank order (and put the new ranking in the "Interim Ranking" column). Then, eliminate the lowest-ranking value (and number it) so you have nine left.

Step 6: Continue to cross off values until you have five left, continuing to number those crossed off. Most of you will find it becomes increasingly difficult to cross values off the closer you come to the final five. Think carefully about the reasons for your decisions about the last three values eliminated.

Values Worksheet	Initial Ranking	Interim Ranking	Final Ranking
Friendship—To work with people I like and who like me.			
Location—To be able to live and work where I want to.			
Enjoyment—To enjoy my work and have fun doing it.			
Loyalty—To be loyal to my company and they to me.			
Family—To have plenty of time with my family.			
Leadership—To become an influential leader in my work.			
Achievement—To accomplish important things in my work and be involved in significant undertakings.			
Self-Realization—To do work that is personally challenging and allows me to achieve the full potential of my talents.			
Wealth—To earn a great deal of money.			
Expertise—To become known and respected as an authority in what I do.			
Service—To contribute to the satisfaction of others.			
Prestige—To be seen as successful; to become well-known.			
Security—To have a secure and stable position at work.			
Power—To have authority to approve or disapprove courses of action and control allocation of resources.			
Independence—To have freedom of thought and action, to be able to control my own schedule and priorities.			
▪			
▪			
▪			

Step 7: Re-rank your values and think about each of them. What does each one mean to you; what about the value appeal to you? When you're satisfied with your ranking, place them in the column, "Final Ranking." Are you achieving these values in your current job (or did you achieve them in your most recent job)? If not, think about what kind of career path or job might help you achieve them.

Step 8: Write your final five values (in rank order). Then write the ten you crossed off with the corresponding numbers so you know the order in which you crossed them off. Look at your final list and think about it, making a mental note of any surprises.

Step 9: On the sheet where you wrote your values, describe any obstacles that you think might prevent you from achieving your values in your next job. Identify each obstacle with the letter B, C, or I, which stand for the following:

✓ Block—It appears impossible to take action to achieve the value.
✓ Constraint—Achieving the value may be possible, but you feel limited in how much you can accomplish without additional resources.
✓ Illusion—Upon further thought, this obstacle is more of my own making and I should be able to overcome it.

At this point, you should have a good sense of what your values are and whether they're realistic given your job possibilities.

3. KNOW YOUR SPIRAL

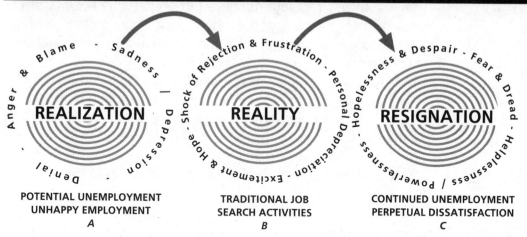

Spiral of Descending Emotions

Anger & Blame - Sadness — Depression - Denial

REALIZATION

Shock of Rejection & Frustration - Personal Depreciation - Excitement & Hope

REALITY

Hopelessness & Despair - Fear & Dread - Helplessness / Powerlessness

RESIGNATION

POTENTIAL UNEMPLOYMENT
UNHAPPY EMPLOYMENT
A

TRADITIONAL JOB
SEARCH ACTIVITIES
B

CONTINUED UNEMPLOYMENT
PERPETUAL DISSATISFACTION
C

The objective of this book is to establish and take control of your career search. In some cases this may involve avoiding or breaking out of the Spiral of Descending Emotions. The Spiral starts with a realization of impending unemployment or of high job dissatisfaction. This leads to the first stage of the spiral: denial, anger, and sadness or depression that can occur early in the traditional job search. In the second stage a job seeker becomes faced with the ups and downs of job search activity: winning interviews and losing out on jobs, the disappointment of rejection, and the resulting personal depreciation. The third stage of the spiral begins with a feeling of helplessness or powerlessness ("Everyone is against me"), which can lead to hopelessness or despair and ultimately dread of any of the job search activities because they only bring rejection. The result is avoidance of the activities altogether and perpetual dissatisfaction or unemployment.

When we embark on a job search, it's just as important to be aware of our emotions as it is to be aware of our values. A lack of awareness can interfere with our ability to perceive employment opportunities correctly; it can drain the energy we need to find a job; it can foster the illusion that we'll never receive a job offer (or the one we want). Most of us get caught in one of the three emotional spirals, and as a result we can't move forward— or we move forward sluggishly or in the wrong direction.

This exercise will help you determine which spiral has you in its grip.

It's not as easy as it sounds. Most of us are out of touch with our emotions at one time or another, and we're especially vulnerable to this problem during a job search. While some of you may be able to spot your spiral by looking at the preceding graphic, others will not. Therefore, let's start with a tool that will facilitate identification.

Make a check mark next to the traits in the following columns that apply to you (the columns correspond to spirals A, B, and C). If you feel uncertain about which ones really apply to you, have someone who knows you well complete this exercise for you. Then, total the check marks for each column. The one with the most checks is the emotional spiral in which you're spinning.

A	B	C
discovered that you are newly unemployed or about to be unemployed ___	realize change is imminent, accepted the need to make a change ___	the search has taken too long ___
become aware of increasing dissatisfaction in your job ___	recognize the need to begin career planning ___	seems like all the good jobs are taken ___
about to be forcibly retired ___	interviews scheduled ___	feels like all the jobs are taken ___
just decided you would like a new job ___	searching the want ads ___	tired of sending letters or applying for jobs ___
arguing ___	asking friends about job openings ___	stopped looking ___
kicking the dog ___	considering going back to school ___	sitting around ___
saying everything is okay ___	mailing letters ___	spend time at the bar ___
saying the change is just a rumor ___	developing/updating resume ___	bills are piling up ___
working harder to save the job ___	visits to the copy center ___	going through the motions of job seeking ___
pointing fingers ___	waiting for callbacks ___	giving up ___
withdrawing from work relationships ___	going for interviews ___	don't prepare for interviews ___
tense up/short fuse ___	receiving rejection letters ___	withdrawing from personal relationships ___
feeling ill ___	working your network ___	become seriously ill ___
crying ___		eat/drink too much ___
excessive sleeping ___		
memorializing ___		

4. EXPRESS YOURSELF

Focus on the emotions that characterize the loop you identified in the previous activity. If you find yourself in either of the first two loops of the spiral, we would highly recommend that you also focus on the remaining loop (or loops) of the spiral. Each of us responds differently to the emotions identified in the spiral. In this activity, your task is to identify how you are likely to respond when experiencing a particular emotion. What would you do or say that would let you and others know your emotional state? If you aren't sure what you would do or say, ask someone who knows you well.

A. Denial ("Say it ain't so, Joe!"):
   In denial, I would do or say ...

B. Anger & Blame ("My boss is such a Bozo. He caused this!"):
   When angry or blaming, I would do or say ...

C. Sadness/Depression ("Maybe I'll just stay in bed today."):
   If sad or depressed, I would do or say ...

D. Excitement & Hope ("I'm perfect for this job!"):
   When excited or hopeful, I would do or say ...

E. Shock/Rejection/Frustration ("How could they pick someone else?"):
   If shocked by rejection or frustrated, I would do or say ...

F. Personal Depreciation ("I've never done anything right!"):
   If I were to put myself down, I would do or say ...

G. Helplessness/Powerlessness ("People like me never get a break."):
   If I felt helpless or powerless, I would do or say ...

H. Hopelessness & Despair ("What's the use anyway?"):
   If I felt hopeless or despairing, I would do or say ...

I. Fear & Dread ("How can I face another interview? This is never going to end."):
   If I experienced fear and dread, I would do or say ...

5. FIND YOUR STICKING POINTS

Whenever we get caught up in negative emotions, we can become stuck. Review the behaviors you identified in the previous exercise and identify specifically how what you are doing or saying could keep you in emotional limbo.

A. Denial could keep me stuck by:
B. Anger & Blame could keep me stuck by:
C. Sadness/Depression could keep me stuck by:
D. Excitement & Hope could keep me stuck by:
E. Shock of Rejection/Frustration could keep me stuck by:
F. Personal Depreciation could keep me stuck by:
G. Helplessness/Powerlessness could keep me stuck by:
H. Hopelessness & Despair could keep me stuck by:
I. Fear & Dread could keep me stuck by:

6. GETTING UNSTUCK

Now it's time to identify ways to break the spiral. Look at the information in the previous three activities, then specify what you feel you need to do to stop going in emotional circles:

I need to stop …
I need to start …
I need to continue …

7. LOOK FOR YOUR BLIND SPOT

Each of us has blind spots when it comes to our own behavior. Show your list to someone you trust and whose opinion you value. Have them review your list and suggest anything that you may have forgotten.

Based on the valued opinions I have received:

I also need to stop …
I also need to start …
I also need to continue …

2
Avoiding Traps and Controlling Your Job Search Direction

Introduction

There are many traps job seekers fall into. In this chapter you will find exercises that will help you avoid them. For instance, you will start out by looking at 18 possible career traps. Some of these may cause you to make a career mistake.

If you find that you are in a trap, many of these exercises will help you work your way out of it.

8. TRY TO FIND YOUR PERSONAL CAREER TRAP

We're all vulnerable to one type of trap or another, especially when we have a job we hate or have no job at all. Instead of dealing with the difficult issues a job search can raise, we fall back on "easy" myths and misconceptions that trap us in the wrong job or field.

Take a look at the following traps and see which one (or ones) apply to you. You'll know you've found one when your head starts to nod or a bell goes off inside it when you read the description of a trap. Make a check mark next to the offending trap and keep this list handy as you search for a job.

1. The "They-told-me-to" Trap: I have a relative who says that I would do well in business, so I am going to go into business.
2. The "Don't-be-different" Trap: I'm a girl, and I really want to be an auto mechanic; but that's a job for men, so I'm going to become a waitress.
3. The "Be-friendly" Trap: My friend is going to work at McDonald's, so I'm going to do the same job because I want to be with my friend.
4. The "Glamour" Trap: I've decided to become a fashion model because they wear a lot of beautiful and expensive clothes.
5. The "Easy-road" Trap: I've decided to go to the XYZ Employment Agency because they find you a job and you don't have to do anything.
6. The "Behind-the-curtain" Trap: I've decided to become an architect. I don't know much about it, but it sounds good.
7. The "I-want-to-look-good" Trap: I've decided to go to college. When I tell people that, they will be impressed.
8. The "I'll-meet-your-needs" Trap: I have a close relative who would be very proud of me if I became a teacher. I don't want to hurt my relative's feelings, so that is what I will become.
9. The "Running-away" Trap: I can't stand being at home. I'm going to get married the first chance that I have.
10. The "Head-in-the-sand" Trap: I didn't do well in math or science, but I've decided to become an engineer because they make good money.
11. The "What's-good-for-you-is-good-for-me" Trap: I know someone who likes being a salesperson, so I've decided to do the same.
12. The "There's-no-tomorrow" Trap: I need as much money as I got before. If I can't get a job here and now that pays it, I'm leaving town.
13. The "All-or-nothing-at-all" Trap: I've decided to be a machinist and nothing else will do.
14. The "Something-will-come-along" Trap: I don't need to do any thinking about a career now. I'll have plenty of time later.
15. The "One-true-love" Trap: I know there is one perfect occupation that is just made for me. I wish I could find it and live happily ever after.
16. The "Start-at-the-top" Trap: I want to be my own boss and have my own business. When I graduate from school (or collect the rest of my unemployment), I'm going to borrow some money and start my own whirligig factory.
17. The "You-know-what's-right-for-me" Trap: I know very little, and you are much wiser than I am. Tell me what to do with my life.
18. The "Grass-is-greener-on-the-other-side" Trap: I don't like this school (or program), so I've decided to go somewhere else.

9. STATE YOUR PREFERENCES

Making Work Wish Lists Come True

Here's a trap that wasn't on the previous list because it's so all-encompassing. It's astonishing how few people really define exactly what they want in a job. Most people tend to stop after they've considered salary and type of position. The activities here are designed to help you identify exactly what work criteria are important to you—everything from the work environment to the level of responsibility to the preferred type of tasks. Just circle your preference on each line:

Work Criteria Preferences

Income adequate to meet living expenses	Income potential unlimited	Doesn't matter
Guaranteed steady income	Commission or pay based on performance	Doesn't matter
Complete benefit package	Benefits not important	Doesn't matter
Employee involvement in management decision making	Top-down management style	Doesn't matter
Short hours: Eight hours per day or less	Long hours and weekend work usual	Doesn't matter
Guaranteed regular hours	Possible overtime	Doesn't matter
Variety of duties every day	Similar duties every day	Doesn't matter
Challenges and risks in work	Work offers security	Doesn't matter
Work for others	Self-employment	Doesn't matter
Large corporation	Small organization	Doesn't matter
Work alone	Work with people	Doesn't matter
Structured environment: Well-defined duties and responsibilities	Unstructured work: Room for creativity and initiative	Doesn't matter
Close supervision	No supervision	Doesn't matter
Low level of responsibility: No critical decisions	High level of responsibility: Make key decisions	Doesn't matter
Many opportunities for advancement and professional development	Few opportunities for advancement and professional development	Doesn't matter
Fast pace, high pressure	Slow pace, low pressure	Doesn't matter
Clearly defined end products: openly achievable goals	Can't necessarily see results of work; long-range goals	Doesn't matter
Requires advanced education	Educational experience unimportant	Doesn't matter
Predominantly indoors	Work outdoors in any weather	Doesn't matter
Sedentary; mostly sitting	Active; requires much movement	Doesn't matter
Perks and extra benefits (car, country club, etc.)	No extra benefits	Doesn't matter
Prestige and status extremely important	Prestige and status are unimportant	Doesn't matter
Close work with machines	Little work with machines	Doesn't matter
Close work with paper	Little work with paper	Doesn't matter
No union involvement	Union representation	Doesn't matter
Organizational commitment to quality	Organizational commitment to production	Doesn't matter
Frequent travel	Little or no travel	Doesn't matter
Early retirement	Work opportunities after 65	Doesn't matter
Live close to work	Live 1/2 hour or more from work	Doesn't matter
Requires previous hands-on experience	Hands-on experience isn't necessary	Doesn't matter
Willing to relocate anywhere	Work in specific geographic area	Doesn't matter

10. CHOOSE YOUR IDEAL WORKING ENVIRONMENT

Each of the following paragraphs offers a first-person description of a working environment. Each one is very different from the others. We'd like you to look over the descriptions and choose the one that comes closest to your ideal. Then, think about that chosen environment and why it's important to you. (Circle your preference.)

1. I prefer work with very clear job direction. I do best when I can work independently to get a task accomplished, without a lot of task interference or interruptions from others. I like working for a supervisor who is decisive and directive. I don't need to know a lot of the "why" on a task, just the "what" that needs to get done. I don't ask a lot of questions. I am not comfortable having to make a lot of independent decisions. I also don't need a lot of social interaction on the job. That can get in the way of my effectiveness.

2. I prefer an environment where my work is somewhat independent, with an occasional opportunity to work with a group or team. I am not totally comfortable in a team environment, but I can make a contribution. I like to know the objectives of the organization so I can see how my effort contributes. I like to take responsibility for my work and have some autonomy in the way it gets done.

3. I prefer an environment where I work very closely with other people, in groups and in teams. I work best when I can exchange a lot of ideas, have a lot of discussion around how to best get something done. It is very important to me to clearly understand what is important to the organization I am part of and how it likes to operate. I appreciate openness and the opportunity to ask my supervisor questions to better understand the work expected. I prefer to be able to share responsibility with my group members in getting work done.

11. WORD ASSOCIATION

Read each phrase below and identify your reaction to that word by circling the + (positive reaction), o (neutral reaction), or – (negative reaction).

Close Supervision	+	o	–
Working with People	+	o	–
Creative Thinking	+	o	–
Writing/Reading Reports	+	o	–
Physical Work	+	o	–
Protecting Information	+	o	–
Taking Action	+	o	–
Building Plans	+	o	–
Analyzing Data	+	o	–
Working Together	+	o	–
Doing Detail Work	+	o	–
Focusing on a Goal	+	o	–
Working Independently	+	o	–
Having Power	+	o	–
Taking Risks	+	o	–
Knowing the Schedule	+	o	–
Schedule Flexibility	+	o	–
Selling Ideas	+	o	–
Knowing the Job Well	+	o	–
Hands-on Work	+	o	–
Repetitive Tasks	+	o	–
Presenting Information	+	o	–
Work Travel	+	o	–
Working at One Location	+	o	–
Taking Accountability	+	o	–

What do your responses indicate to you about the type of environment you would like to work in and the type of work you like to do?

_____

_____

_____

_____

_____

12. CHOOSE YOUR ORGANIZATIONAL CULTURE

This table provides some contrast between different types of organizations. Review the descriptive words to help validate which type of organization you would be most comfortable in. Circle the column that comes closest to your comfort zone.

Tell-Oriented	*Involve-Oriented*	*Team-Oriented*
directive	friendly	participative
pushy	questioning	sharing
one-way communication	groupwork	fun
urgent	thinking invited	social
get it done!	independent	teamwork
the boss rules	asking	problem solving
finger pointing	personal accountability	team thinking required
not social	discussion	vision
quiet	flexible	autonomous
management decides		delegation
fixed ways		team responsibility
		open decision making

13. FINDING YOUR JOB COMFORT ZONE

Some of us never find satisfying work because we have a perfect job or career fixed in our minds and we refuse to compromise with perfection. While it's sometimes helpful to dream about ideal jobs, it can be counterproductive if we refuse to accept anything else.

The purpose of this exercise is to let you determine what's a reasonable compromise. How much good stuff and how much bad stuff can we really tolerate? Where is your job comfort zone?

Start by listing a characteristic you would love in a job. Then, consider how much of that characteristic would be too much or too little, and then, determine the realistic range. Here is an example:

Things I would love in a job	How much is too much?	How much is not enough?	Realistic range
Travel to other locations	20 nights away	2 nights away	4-10 nights away
Use of my problem-solving skills	All the time	Never	Several problems a week

Now it is your turn. After you work on the things you would love,
list the things you would hate.

Things I would love in a job	How much is too much?	How much is not enough?	Realistic range
Things I would hate in a job	What is the most I could tolerate?	What is the minimum I could expect?	Realistic range

3

Leveraging Accomplishments

Introduction

Most of us doubt our accomplishments. We just don't think we've accomplished very much. When asked what we've achieved in our work lives, many of us can do no more than shrug our shoulders. In fact, we've all accomplished far more than we think. It's just that when we're dissatisfied with our jobs or out of work, we tend to downplay our accomplishments ..or we prefer to dwell on what we haven't achieved rather than on what we have.

In this chapter, you'll find activities that will remind you of all the things that distinguish you. As you'll see, the exercises aren't merely designed to identify obvious accomplishments—promotions, raises, and other perks. Instead, they'll give you a sense of your special abilities, based on what you've done in the past. Everyone demonstrates talent in at least one area of life—sometimes in many areas. Everyone has done something worthy of recognition—scored the winning touchdown, won an art competition, done charitable work.

Sometimes we separate our personal lives from our professional lives, our nonwork accomplishments from our work ones. But it's important to think about our achievements holistically— skills frequently translate well from one area of life to another. The activities in this chapter should give you a good idea of what you've accomplished and how those accomplishments might help you in finding a satisfying job or career.

14. LIFELINE

The line on the following page represents your lifeline from birth to today. On the line, identify the six or seven most significant events, experiences, or milestones (positive or negative) that have helped you become the individual you are today.

These should be milestones that contributed significantly to your personal development and present capabilities. Some examples of significant events would be attending college classes, a special work assignment, a specific job, failing to get into the college of your choice, or going to vocational school. If your current search is the result of a recent job loss or layoff, designate that as one of your significant events.

Considering the left side of the line to be your birth and the right side of the line to be today, identify the point or area of the line for each of these significant events. Then, write the name of your positive experiences above the line and your negative experiences below the line. Number each experience and note what you learned from each one in the note space at the bottom of the page.

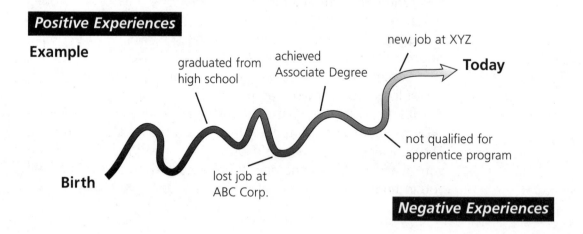

Positive Experiences

Example

new job at XYZ

Today

graduated from high school

achieved Associate Degree

not qualified for apprentice program

Birth

lost job at ABC Corp.

Negative Experiences

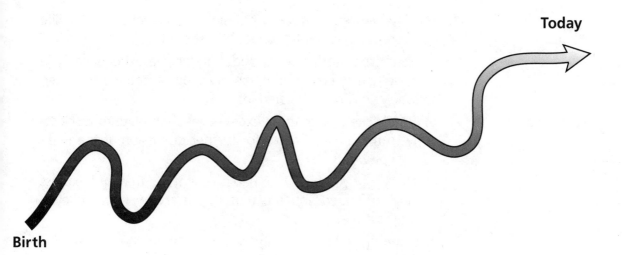

Today

Birth

What I Learned:

1.	2.	3.	4.
5.	6.	7.	8.

15. QUICK QUIZ—THE WEIRDEST JOB INTERVIEW YOU'LL NEVER HAVE

We'd like you to pretend you're in a job interview with an interviewer who asks a number of unusual questions. Feel free to have a friend ask you these questions, if it makes this exercise easier. The key is to articulate your experiences.

1. The interviewer asks you what significant events in your life have prepared you for this job. You should:
   a. Start from age three and identify all the experiences you have had to ensure that you bring up something the interviewer will be interested in.
   b. Briefly cite two or three experiences that relate most closely to this job and allow for further discussion, if the interviewer wants.
   c. Deny that you have ever had an event like that and express how offended you are that the interviewer would even suggest that you did.

2. In communicating your significant event to the interviewer, you should:
   a. Convey a deeply personal and emotional experience that is likely to bring tears to the interviewer's eyes.
   b. Become so personally moved in the telling of this event to the interviewer that you are unable to continue the interview.
   c. Communicate the event(s) in a straightforward manner and identify what you learned from the event(s) in an upbeat way.

3. In choosing the significant event(s) to discuss, the best ones would be:
   a. Recent: Like one about the child's birthday party you attended last week and how a carbonated beverage got sprayed all over you.
   b. Early in your life, like high school stories.
   c. About other people you know.
   d. Professional and personal stories that demonstrate your capabilities and character.

The best answer for 1 is B; for 2 is C, and for 3 is D.

A final bit of advice: Explore the way you communicate your significant life events. Are you sharing information in a way that impresses the interviewer with your character and your abilities? If you were the interviewer, would you think this particular event qualifies you for a job? Until we verbalize significant life experiences, we don't know how to communicate them so that they have a positive impact on others. So, even if you feel a little silly at first, try to talk it out, rather than think it out.

16. SIGNIFICANT EXPERIENCES

Try it here. Write down a couple of your significant experiences. Then answer the questions that follow each of them.

Significant Experience
What did you learn from the experience?
How does that experience bring value to a prospective employer?
Significant Experience
What did you learn from the experience?
How does that experience bring value to a prospective employer?

17. ALIEN ENCOUNTER

You have decided to apply to be a member of an expeditionary team whose mission is establishing successful contact with beings from another planet. Every position on the team is expected to bring unique skills and talents to the mission. Many functions will have to be performed to ensure the success of this encounter.

Choose a role from the list below that best suits you and your skills. If you can't find a role that fits, create one that describes what your contribution would be. At Step Two, assume you are preparing for your interview and identify which key personal characteristics make you the best candidate for that role on the team. Step Three asks you to list your strategy for communicating those characteristics to the interviewer.

Step One—Choose or identify a role.

Researcher	Communications Coordinator
Computer Programmer	Translator
Counselor	Navigator
Equipment Operator	Supply Officer/Quartermaster
Ambassador	Logistics Coordinator
Administrative Coordinator	Mission Commander
Medic	Morale Officer
Engineer	Systems Analyst
Mechanical Officer	Galley Officer
Other: _____	

Step Two—Define the characteristics that make you the best candidate for that role.

_____

_____

_____

_____

_____

_____

_____

Step Three—Determine how you will communicate those characteristics in your interview.

_____

_____

_____

_____

_____

_____

_____

_____

18. THINGS TO DO WITH ACCOMPLISHMENTS

Up to this point, the activities in this chapter have been designed to make you more aware of significant events and experiences in your life and how they might be useful in a job or career search. Now we're going to focus on your specific accomplishments and how they translate into marketable job skills. Let's start with the following exercise:

A. My Greatest Accomplishments

After the earlier exercises, you should be able to write your greatest accomplishments in the following eight areas. As you're doing so, we'd like you to add three other thoughts: what motivated you to accomplish what you did, what kind of feedback you received, and what your feelings were about what you achieved.

My Greatest Accomplishments

1. My greatest accomplishment with my family:

2. My greatest accomplishment in school:

3. My greatest accomplishment on a job:

4. My greatest accomplishment with friends:

5. My greatest accomplishment in the community:

6. My greatest accomplishment in the arts or hobbies:

7. My greatest accomplishment alone:

8. Any other accomplishments of which I'm very proud:

19. TURNING ACCOMPLISHMENTS INTO SKILLS

In the previous activity, one of the eight accomplishments you listed had to do with work. Now try to create a much longer list of work-related peak accomplishments on the accompanying worksheet. Include everything from achieving a team objective to coming up with a great new idea.

After you've completed your list, make a check mark next to those accomplishments for which you really enjoyed the work involved.

Finally, review the Skill List, and write the skill you used for each accomplishment on the worksheet.

Focus on the checked accomplishments and the corresponding skills. Find a job that requires these skills, and you'll probably find a job you'll enjoy.

Skill List	
1. Analyzing information	11. Performing repetitive tasks
2. Checking completeness/accuracy of work	12. Planning work of others
3. Communicating orally	13. Organizing information/tasks
4. Communicating in writing	14. Solving complex problems
5. Coordinating people, places, meetings	15. Managing multiple tasks
6. Dealing with customers/public	16. Working under minimal supervision
7. Developing new or improved procedures	17. Working under pressure
8. Expediting results	18. Working within deadlines
9. Initiating ideas	19. Working with abstract ideas
10. Instructing others	20. Working with figures

Peak Accomplishments Worksheet

Peak Accomplishment	✓	Skills
▪		
▪		
▪		
▪		
▪		
▪		
▪		
▪		

4

Know Thyself, Sell Thyself

Introduction

We hope the activities in the previous chapter demonstrated that you've accomplished more than you might have thought—in both your personal and professional life. You also identified skills related to accomplishments. In this chapter, you'll develop a greater understanding of the specific skills you possess. Each exercise is an entertaining journey of self-discovery, a painless way to figure out your unique mix of competencies. The better you know yourself, the better you'll sell yourself.

20. SKILL SELECTING

In the previous chapter, you listed the skills suggested by your peak accomplishments. Here, we'd like you to complete the following worksheet by (a) writing the number of times you wrote down each listed skill in the peak accomplishments exercise, (b) ranking the top five skills based on enjoyment (what skills you like using most, down to the ones you like using least), and (c) placing a check mark next to the skills you hope to use most in the next five to ten years.

Skill Inventory	Strength	Rank	5-10
1. Analyzing information			
2. Checking completeness/accuracy of work			
3. Communicating orally			
4. Communicating in writing			
5. Coordinating people, places, meetings			
6. Dealing with customers/public			
7. Developing new or improved procedures			
8. Expediting results			
9. Initiating ideas			
10. Instructing others/facilitating			
11. Performing repetitive tasks			
12. Planning work of others			
13. Organizing information/tasks			
14. Solving complex problems			
15. Managing multiple tasks			
16. Working under minimal supervision			
17. Working under pressure			
18. Working within deadlines			
19. Working with abstract ideas			
20. Working with figures			
21. Other:			
22. Other:			

21. ATTRIBUTES: A TO Z

A more sophisticated way of analyzing our skills involves looking at them within the context of attributes—the personal qualities that influence how we use the skills we have. We've listed 32 common attributes in alphabetical order. Determine whether you seldom, sometimes, or almost always employ that attribute in your work.

Attributes Worksheet	Seldom	Some-times	Almost Always
Able to work alone. Do you plan your own work? Can you work by yourself when there are no other people around?			
Aggressive. Do you promote a course of action or an assignment energetically? Do you often take the initiative?			
Ambitious. Do you keep up with the current literature in your profession? Do you take on extra assignments that will help you get ahead? Do you plan your career advancement?			
Analytical. Do you perceive relationships easily? Have you ever solved a problem that had others baffled?			
Articulate. Can you express ideas easily—verbally or in writing? Are your instructions readily understood?			
Cheerful. Are you generally good-natured? Do you greet your fellow workers pleasantly?			
Competent. Are you able to meet deadlines? Is your work generally accepted "as is"? Have you ever accomplished some feat of speed or skill in your chosen field?			
Congenial. Do you work well with others? Have you volunteered to cheerfully serve on committees at school; at work; in the community?			
Conscientious. Do you do an honest day's work for a day's pay? Can you name some unpleasant task you have done because it had to be done and no one else would do it?			
Cooperative. Do you always do your part in a team assignment? Do you often volunteer to help?			
Courageous. Do you undertake challenges readily? Have you ever had to stand firm on your principles, despite opposition?			
Courteous. Do you treat your fellow workers with respect? Observe the common sense rules of social behavior?			
Decisive. Are you able to make clear-cut decisions under pressure? Do you stand behind them later? Can you take a firm stand and accept responsibility for it?			
Dependable. How is your attendance record? Can your supervisor count on you when the workload is heavy? Do you follow through, without being checked on by your supervisor or instructors?			
Diplomatic. Can you cope with difficult situations involving other people? Have you restored harmony where there was friction; settled a difficult personnel problem?			
Discreet. Are you able to keep a secret? Do you guard confidential material carefully? Do you respect other people's right to privacy?			
Efficient. Do you plan your time well? Do you consciously try to improve your work habits to more easily get your job done?			
Emotionally Stable. Do you feel in control of yourself most of the time? Can other people count in your day-to-day mood to be generally agreeable? Do you ordinarily feel good toward other people?			

Attributes Worksheet	Seldom	Some-times	Almost Always
Enthusiastic. Are you interested in your work or studies? Do you inspire others with your own interest? Are you often "high energy" because of your excitement about your job? Have you ever done extra work because of your interest?			
Honest. Have you ever served as a treasurer of an organization; been bonded? Are you careful with trade secrets; school or company property and supplies? Do you pass along the praise when credit belongs elsewhere? Do you accept blame for your own mistakes?			
Imaginative. Do you often or occasionally come up with new ideas? Have you ever contributed an idea that proved both workable and profitable? Do you let yourself have the freedom to be creative and dream up new ways of doing things?			
Industrious. Are you your own self-starter? Do you work steadily on a task until it is done? Do you resist interruptions whenever possible?			
Judicious. Can you sift evidence and arrive at a sound judgment? Are you able to separate your emotions from your sense of logic? Have you ever made a decision based on reason when it conflicted with your emotional interests?			
Leadership Ability. Do people willingly follow your suggestions? Have you held positions of responsibility at work; in school; in clubs; in community activities?			
Loyal. Can you set aside petty grievances to get a job done? Have you ever been in a situation where you stayed with a project or organization because of a sense of responsibility, despite disagreements?			
Observant. Do you remember names and places easily? Do you recall facts and figures accurately; find your way in a new locale?			
Open-minded. Are you able to accept ideas contrary to your own? Do you adapt well to change?			
Orderly. Do you keep things where they belong; have a knack for arranging things in a logical way; enjoy detail work?			
Patient. Can you keep your temper? Are you often bored with the work you are doing? Are you able to train others calmly, even when you have to explain some procedures over and over again?			
Studious. Do you constantly think about how to do your work better? Do you read up on information about your job?			
Watchful. Do you keep an eye open for problems? Do you listen for ways to prevent problems or improve quality? Do you look for ways to help others?			
Zealous. Do you maintain a high level of energy? Can you share that energy with others? Are you able to put 110% into your work?			

22. WORKING WITH STYLE: WHICH ONE FITS YOU?

Your personal style has a significant impact on how employers perceive you—and whether they hire you. It also affects how well you do in a given job. Some positions are tailor-made for your particular style, while others clash with it. Many of us don't have a clear sense of our style, and as a result we do poorly in interviews or take jobs we should run from. This activity and the two that follow will help you see yourself as others see you—a critical asset for any job seeker.

Interpersonal Style Rating Scale*

Instructions: Listed below are words and phrases that people use to describe themselves and others. Beside each word or phrase, fill in the circle that corresponds to *your perception of how you think others see you.* Use the example below to guide you in indicating the degree to which that word or phrase describes you.

EXAMPLE:

Calm

Not at all descriptive ① ② ③ ④ ⑤ ⑥ ⑦ Very descriptive

If you believe others see you as *not at all* calm, you should fill in the number 1 circle. If you believe that others see you as *very* calm, fill in the number 7 circle. If you are seen somewhere in between, fill in the circle that best indicates your perception. Before starting, please also read the special guidelines.

Now, do the same for the adjectives and phrases on the following page. *Please respond to every word or phrase, even if you are not certain.*

Important: Please Read Before Beginning the Exercise

The scales are based on the assumption that ordinary language provides a sufficient basis for describing behavior. They also assume that language is redundant, i.e., fewer words are needed than are often used. The words and phrases in our reference sampling have been chosen to communicate best the meanings of the scales, and the scales have been researched to establish homogeneity. As you look at each word or phrase, think of the perceptions that exist between yourself and a particular group of people you (typically) work with, for example: customers, coworkers, suppliers, or subordinates. Consider the relationships in terms of the day-to-day tasks in which you are (or were) involved.

---

*The *Interpersonal Style Profile*, and the information contained in *Interpreting Your Score* and *Dimensions of Interpersonal Style* are © International Learning 1991. All rights reserved. Adapted and used with permission.

Group D

aggressive	① ② ③ ④ ⑤ ⑥ ⑦	_____
challenging/ confronting	① ② ③ ④ ⑤ ⑥ ⑦	_____
forceful	① ② ③ ④ ⑤ ⑥ ⑦	_____
outspoken	① ② ③ ④ ⑤ ⑥ ⑦	_____
takes charge	① ② ③ ④ ⑤ ⑥ ⑦	_____
assertive	① ② ③ ④ ⑤ ⑥ ⑦	_____
competitive	① ② ③ ④ ⑤ ⑥ ⑦	_____
straightforward	① ② ③ ④ ⑤ ⑥ ⑦	_____
frank	① ② ③ ④ ⑤ ⑥ ⑦	_____
blunt	① ② ③ ④ ⑤ ⑥ ⑦	_____
	D =	_____

Group S

accepting/ supporting	① ② ③ ④ ⑤ ⑥ ⑦	_____
easy to know	① ② ③ ④ ⑤ ⑥ ⑦	_____
friendly/outgoing	① ② ③ ④ ⑤ ⑥ ⑦	_____
people-oriented	① ② ③ ④ ⑤ ⑥ ⑦	_____
sociable	① ② ③ ④ ⑤ ⑥ ⑦	_____
agreeable	① ② ③ ④ ⑤ ⑥ ⑦	_____
cares how others feel	① ② ③ ④ ⑤ ⑥ ⑦	_____
flexible	① ② ③ ④ ⑤ ⑥ ⑦	_____
warm	① ② ③ ④ ⑤ ⑥ ⑦	_____
fun-loving	① ② ③ ④ ⑤ ⑥ ⑦	_____
	S =	_____

Instructions for Scoring

1. Place the number you have circled in the blank space to the right of each row.
2. Total your score for Group D.
3. Total your score for Group S.
4. Compare the sum for each group to the appropriate "key" shown below.

5. Place an "X" in the proper quadrant in the chart below.

Group D Total _____   **Group S Total** _____

Key: 56-70 = A   **Key:** 00-46 = 1
         51-55 = B   47-52 = 2
         46-50 = C   53-57 = 3
         00-45 = D   58-70 = 4

Circle your combined letter and number score:

A-1	A-2	A-3	A-4	B-1	B-2	B-3	B-4
C-1	C-2	C-3	C-4	D-1	D-2	D-3	D-4

	D	C	B	A	
1					
P4					**P1**
2					
3					
P3					**P2**
4					

What Your Scores Mean*

You've just completed a psychologically-based inventory designed by International Learning, Inc. You can use it to categorize your verbal and nonverbal interactions with others. You pick up clues about a person by his or her behaviors—a smile, a sigh, a tone of voice, a clenched fist, and so on. It's not what a person says that determines style, but the way that person says it and "shows" it.

To understand your interpersonal style based on this inventory, you need to understand what your Group D Score (Dominance) and Group S Score (Sociability) mean.

*The *Interpersonal Style Profile,* and the information contained in *Interpreting Your Score* and *Dimensions of Interpersonal Style* are © International Learning 1991. All rights reserved. Adapted and used with permission.

Whether we consciously realize it or not, all of us are observers of the human scene. We have conditioned ourselves to pick up clues from the overt behavior of others—a smile, a frown, a deep sigh, a clenching of the fist, a shaking of the head, a gaze. We also tend to send signals to others in a variety of ways—a glance away, a crossing of the arms or legs, a hearty laugh, leaning back, leaning forward, and countless other actions that may indicate a person's degree of *Dominance* (Group D score) and *Sociability* (Group S score) in a relationship. The signals we send to each other are observed and catalogued in our minds. Very often they determine our likely actions and reactions toward each other.

The respective acts we choose are usually consistent with the set of behaviors we feel most comfortable with—our "comfort zones." Over time, these behaviors become habitual, and they comprise the Interpersonal Style we use in dealing with others.

Dimensions of Interpersonal Style*

✓ **Dominance is a measurement of a person's effort to influence the thinking and actions of others.** At one extreme, high dominance, are individuals who tend to attempt to influence others through overt, personal control. At the other extreme, low dominance, are those individuals who assert themselves with moderate, unassuming, and quiet behaviors.

✓ **Sociability is the tendency to express feelings openly and to be outgoing with people.** At one extreme, high sociability, are those behaviors that indicate a high display of feelings and emotions in one's interactions. At the other extreme, low sociability, a person tends to show a minimum, outward display of feelings and emotions.

Four Distinct Styles

Those individuals whose scores fall anywhere within quadrant P-1 display varying degrees of High Dominance and Low Sociability. We refer to these individuals as **Drivers.**

Those individuals whose scores fall anywhere within quadrant P-2 display varying degrees of Low Dominance and High Sociability. We refer to these individuals as **Amiables.**

Individuals whose scores fall anywhere within quadrant P-3 display varying degrees of High Dominance and High Sociability. These individuals are known as **Expressives.**

Individuals whose scores fall anywhere within quadrant P-4 display varying degrees of Low Dominance and Low Sociability. These individuals are known as **Analyticals.**

Drivers are strong-willed, independent, and goal-oriented. They are swift to react and direct in the way they act, saying exactly what's on their minds. They are driven by action and can't stand inaction. They think in terms of the here-and-now and like to take control of situations.

Expressives are ambitious, stimulating, dramatic, and friendly. They react rapidly and tend to act impulsively, driven by their "gut instincts." They think in terms of the future possibilities and want to be involved with others.

Amiables are supportive, dependable, agreeable and respectful of others. They react in an unhurried fashion. They are driven by the desire to relate to others and therefore, tend to reject conflict. Like the drivers, they think in the here-and-now; but, unlike the drivers, they devote little effort to effect change.

Analyticals are by no means antisocial. They are industrious, persistent, orderly, and detailed. They are slow to react and cautious in taking action, relying heavily on data and precedence to make decisions. Being thought-driven, analyticals' thinking relies on a historical perspective, drawing on the past and their data to organize the present and the future.

The thumbnail sketches of the four styles by no means do them justice. In reality, all of us use elements of all four style types in varying combinations, which contribute to our individual differences. Each of the four styles mentioned here is routinely subdivided into four substyles of its own (which accounts for the sixteen boxes within the four-quadrant chart). For a detailed understanding of personal styles and this particular system of understanding behavioral diversity, we would recommend you seek out *Personal Styles & Effective Performance* by David W. Merrill and Roger H. Reid (© 1981, Chilton Book Company). For now, we'll stick with the four basic styles and try to apply them in our search for self-discovery in the following two activities.

23. FIND THE STRENGTHS IN YOUR STYLE

Find your personal style from the previous activity. Review the thumbnail sketch of that particular style. In the chart below, list all the adjectives you can think of that would describe that style in the left-hand column. At this point, don't worry about whether the adjective has a positive or negative connotation.

Adjectives	Strengths	Potentials

Review your list of adjectives. Place a "+" next to any adjective you see as positive. Rewrite your positives in the middle column, the Strengths column.

Those adjectives that remain are not your negatives. On the contrary, they represent overused strengths. For example, *pushiness* is really assertiveness overused (too intense). Reread the adjectives that do not have a "+" next to them. If each of those remaining adjectives was "less intense," what other word would come to mind to replace it? If the new word does not already appear in your Strengths column, place it in the remaining column as a Potential.

You can use these adjectives, along with numerous other "power words," to describe yourself to a potential employer in resumes and interviews, but we'll discuss that in later chapters.

24. TRANSLATING YOUR STYLE INTO WORK BEHAVIORS

We hazard a guess that most employers would want to know more than what adjectives best describe you. Those descriptive adjectives you just identified need to be translated into behavior on the job.

Take another look at your identified personal style, the thumbnail sketch, and the adjectives you identified in the previous activity. Your challenge in this activity is to translate that information into statements of behavior that an employer can actually use.

For example, looking at the characteristics of a driver, one might say that as a driver you can ...

✓ work independently
✓ get the job done
✓ complete tasks on time
✓ provide direction to others
✓ accept challenges

We can say for the other styles:

Expressives—work well with others, think creatively, are visionary

Amiables—are good team members, achieve consensus, do the job

Analyticals—attend to detail, organize and plan, think things through*

*For a detailed discussion of the four styles, their work preferences, and how to better relate to the other styles, we would again recommend the Merrill and Reid book previously referenced.

In the space below, think of as many behavioral statements as you can to describe yourself and your personal style. Make sure you go beyond just repeating your adjectives; use them to describe work-related behavior:

■
■
■
■
■
■
■

25. CHOOSE YOUR POWER WORDS

Some of the following 152 words describe you perfectly. The goal here is for you to search for and circle the ones that do so. Not only will this exercise give you additional insights about your strengths, but it will also give you a vocabulary to describe them when talking with people who might hire you. After you've circled your words, complete the two mini-exercises that follow to help you refine your list and show you how they apply in work situations.

Academic	Dignified	Logical	Retiring
Accurate	Discreet	Loyal	Robust
Active	Dominant	Mature	Self-confident
Adaptable	Eager	Methodical	Self-controlled
Adventurous	Easy-going	Meticulous	Sensible
Affectionate	Efficient	Mild	Sensitive
Alert	Emotional	Moderate	Serious
Ambitious	Energetic	Modest	Sharp-witted
Artistic	Enterprising	Natural	Sincere
Assertive	Enthusiastic	Obliging	Sociable
Attractive	Fair-minded	Open-minded	Spontaneous
Bold	Farsighted	Opportunistic	Spunky
Broad-minded	Firm	Optimistic	Stable
Businesslike	Flexible	Organized	Steady
Calm	Forceful	Original	Strong
Capable	Formal	Outgoing	Strong-minded
Careful	Frank	Painstaking	Sympathetic
Caring	Friendly	Patient	Tactful
Cautious	Generous	Peaceable	Teachable
Charming	Gentle	Persevering	Tenacious
Cheerful	Good-natured	Pleasant	Thorough
Clear-thinking	Healthy	Poised	Thoughtful
Clever	Helpful	Polite	Tolerant
Competent	Honest	Practical	Tough
Competitive	Humorous	Precise	Trusting
Confident	Idealistic	Progressive	Trustworthy
Conscientious	Imaginative	Prudent	Unaffected
Conservative	Independent	Quick	Unassuming
Considerate	Individualistic	Quiet	Understanding
Cool	Industrious	Rational	Unexcitable
Cooperative	Informal	Realistic	Uninhibited
Courageous	Ingenious	Reasonable	Verbal
Creative	Intelligent	Reflective	Versatile
Curious	Inventive	Relaxed	Warm
Deliberate	Kind	Reliable	Wholesome
Democratic	Leisurely	Reserved	Wise
Dependable	Lighthearted	Resourceful	Witty
Determined	Likable	Responsible	Zany

In the spaces below, write ten of the previously identified strength words that you believe best describe you.

1. _____ 2. _____

3. _____ 4. _____

5. _____ 6. _____

7. _____ 8. _____

9. _____ 10. _____

These are some of the qualities that you will be selling to employers. Now take three of these words and write examples to describe how you used these strengths in a work situation.

1. Power Word: _____

   Work Situation: _____

   _____

2. Power Word: _____

   Work Situation: _____

   _____

3. Power Word: _____

   Work Situation: _____

   _____

26. SEEING YOURSELF THROUGH OTHERS' EYES

Sometimes we fool ourselves into thinking we possess skills we lack, or we fail to perceive our most significant attributes and focus on relatively minor ones. While an outside observer may not know us as well as we know ourselves, the collective observations of friends, family, and work associates can provide the objectivity we may be missing.

Don't worry. We're not going to suggest you ask 20 people to provide you with their observations. Instead, we'd like you to imagine what they might say about you. How would they describe your strengths?

Place yourself in the following situation. You are finishing a job interview and think things are going well. The interviewer asks you to list the following types of references. In the space at the right, list the name of the individual you recommend they contact in each category:

Relative	
Best friend	
Most recent employer	
First employer	
A teacher	
Someone else of your choosing	

Each of the references you recommended was called. Each person was asked the exact same questions, and each gave a response. In the space below, indicate what you think each of your references said in response to the following questions:

1. What is the one quality you (the job candidate) possess that no one else applying for the job does?
2. What is the one thing you (the job candidate) need to work on to improve your value to the company if hired?

Relative:	1. _____
	2. _____
Best friend:	1. _____
	2. _____
Last employer:	1. _____
	2. _____
First employer:	1. _____
	2. _____
Teacher:	1. _____
	2. _____
Your choice:	1. _____
	2. _____

Review the responses you think your references would give. Are there any themes you can identify among either your strengths or weaknesses?

Themes:

As you review the responses you think your references would give, think about what you could do to:

1. Build upon your strengths?

2. Overcome your weaknesses?

27. SO YOU WANNA BE A ...

When we were younger, many of us had fantasies of exotic careers—secret agent, ball player, astronaut, lion tamer, just to name a few. Sadly, as we grew older, we became more realistic—accountant, engineer, lawyer, teacher, technician, etc.

As we turn our attention to traditional careers, our ideas of the skills we need to develop also take on a more traditional focus. But is there something we can learn from our childhood dreams that can serve us as adults? What if we have some skills that we don't necessarily think we can apply in nontraditional settings?

In the space below, read the jobs listed and identify at least three skills you currently possess that you could bring to each job if you were to apply for it. Then answer the questions that follow.

Actor/actress
Aircraft controller
Rodeo clown
Soccer/football/baseball/hockey player
Talk show/game show host(ess)
Trivia expert

a. Look at the skills you identified. Are there any skills you possess that you hadn't previously identified?

_____

_____

_____

_____

_____

b. How can you apply these skills to the traditional careers you are considering?

_____

_____

_____

_____

_____

c. What skills would you like to develop?

_____

_____

_____

_____

_____

II

TARGETING YOUR MARKET

5
Choosing Your Job Instead of Letting It Choose You

Introduction

You've heard the expression "beggars can't be choosers." Most job seekers find themselves in the position of beggars, happily accepting whatever is available or offered. Needless to say, this is not what we would call a strategic job search. Though sometimes we desperately need a job and can't afford to be picky, most of the time we don't give ourselves much choice. Have you ever sat down and really thought about all the things you really wanted (or didn't want) in a job? Have you ever created an ideal dream job to shoot for or considered what tasks and skills really give you pleasure?

Here's your chance.

28. MULTIPLE CHOICE—TEST WHAT'S REALLY IMPORTANT TO YOU

This is the only multiple choice quiz for which all the answers are correct—as long as they're your answers. We've created questions in a variety of categories designed to help you identify what's critically important to you, versus what's of relatively minor importance—knowing these things will help you gain more control of where and how you work. In an earlier chapter, you had the chance to select work preference criteria; this quiz is a similar tool, but one that allows you to pinpoint the factors that can make or break a job.

1. Financial compensation is:
   a. The single most important factor in a job.
   b. Important, but I'd take a lower salary for other benefits.
   c. Somewhat important, but not as critical as opportunities to learn new skills and gain satisfaction from the job.
   d. Not very important.

2. Decision-making responsibility is:
   a. Essential; I wouldn't accept a job without it.
   b. Something I enjoy, though I don't mind others making certain decisions for me.
   c. A task that others generally like more than me; I prefer to do, rather than decide.
   d. Not an issue I'd even consider.

3. I am willing to work:
   a. As many hours as are necessary to get the job done, including nights and weekends.
   b. From 40 to 60 hours a week regularly.
   c. From 40 to 60 hours a week occasionally.
   d. No more than 40 hours a week.

4. I prefer a work environment that is:
   a. Unstructured and flexible—one that allows me to determine where, how, and when I do my work.

b. Reasonably flexible and without the close supervision and rules that characterized work environments in the past.

c. Structured, though there are opportunities to work in new and different ways when appropriate.

d. Highly structured.

5. I prefer a work environment that is:

  a. High-pressured with tight deadlines.

  b. Intense but with reasonable deadlines.

  c. Moderate pressure with occasional deadlines.

  d. Relaxed with few deadlines.

6. When it comes to the work itself, I like:

  a. Tasks that require creativity and out-of-the-box thinking.

  b. A mix of challenging and routine assignments.

  c. A few challenging projects but mostly tasks that I feel comfortable with and know how to do.

  d. Responsibilities that are familiar and easy for me to perform well.

7. I prefer to work for a company that's:

  a. One of the most prestigious in the world.

  b. Among the leaders in its industry.

  c. One that's small enough so that everyone knows everyone else and people don't get lost.

  d. Size and status don't matter as long as it's a good place to work.

8. I most enjoy working:

  a. On my own with no or little supervision.

  b. Sometimes on my own and sometimes with others.

  c. With close supervision, the assistance of subordinates, or both.

  d. On teams.

9. I would like to work in a job where travel is:

   a. Constant.

   b. Occasional.

   c. Infrequent.

   d. Not required.

10. The type of organization I want to work for will base promotions and compensation primarily on:

   a. Individual performance.

   b. Team performance.

   c. A mixture of individual and team performance.

   d. Factors such as seniority and loyalty.

29. WANTED: THE PERFECT JOB

Now that you've quizzed yourself, try describing the ideal job that's the sum of all your quiz answers. It's not easy to do, is it? When we add up all the different elements that make a job meaningful, it's hard to articulate the result.

To help you do so, imagine yourself as the Human Resources Manager of an organization that is advertising for your perfect job. The activity here is for you to write the want ad for this job. Feel free to review your responses to other exercises in previous chapters, such as the list of skills you created in the first chapter. Start out by answering the following questions:

✓ What are the major duties of this job (tasks during a typical day)?

✓ What skills are necessary to do this job (technical skills, people skills, etc.)?

✓ What education and experience would the best candidate for the job have?

✓ What makes the job attractive?

✓ What opportunities are there for advancement for the person who is chosen for the job?

✓ What type of individual is needed to fill the position (personal qualities and values)?

✓ What is a realistic salary range and what are the associated benefits?

✓ What type of company is offering the job (a leader in the industry, a small firm, etc.)?

Based on your responses, write a detailed want ad for the position. It may help you to look at the want ads in the paper (though some of you are probably quite familiar with them if you've been out of work for awhile). After you've written your ad, keep it handy when you're trying to decide whether to apply for or accept a position. Though it's unlikely that a real job will match your ideal description, the strategic search process we advocate encourages you to search for a position that comes close.

Position:
Major Duties:
Education & Experience Required:
Job Attractors & Opportunities:
Personal Qualities Desired:
Salary & Benefits:
Company Description:

30. FROM FANTASY TO REALITY

When we were younger (or maybe even now), we had fantasies of exotic and incredible careers. We dreamed of being professional athletes, movie stars, and other roles that would bring us fame, fortune or happiness. Most of us, however, have had to temper our dreams with reality.

At the same time, we shouldn't dismiss these fantasies. Many of them hold the key to what we're really searching for in a career. To make educated career and job choices, we need to be aware of our dreams. While we may not be the next superstar athlete or movie star, it's not too late to identify what it is in those fantasies that appeals to us. Many "ordinary" jobs require the same skills that extraordinary ones demand. Finding a job that offers you the chance to use these skills will probably make work a much more satisfying experience.

We've listed some common dream jobs or professions below. Take a look at this list, add to it if you would like, and place a check mark next to the jobs you were attracted to when you were at the different ages in the columns. Then, identify what it was that attracted you to each of those professions.

	under 10	11 to 15	16 to 21	Attraction
Movie Star				
Astronaut				
Doctor				
Cowboy				
Soldier				
Teacher				
Scientist				
Veterinarian				
Firefighter				
Circus Performer				
Fashion Model				

	under 10	11 to 15	16 to 21	Attraction
Politician				
Police Officer				
Professional Athlete				
Builder				
Lawyer				
Inventor				
Truck Driver				
Auto Mechanic				
Fashion Designer				

a. Now think about the attraction for each of those professions. How do they relate to your interests today?

_____

_____

_____

b. What interests do you possess that are similar to the careers you were once interested in?

_____

_____

_____

c. Which interests would you like to leverage into your next position?

_____

_____

_____

31. WORST-CASE SCENARIOS

Sometimes we can learn as much from nightmare jobs as we can from dream ones. Recognizing the type of working environments we despise will help us avoid getting stuck in them. This exercise gives you choices between two extremes. Your assignment is to choose (by circling) the one that really makes you cringe.

The worst boss I could possibly have would be one who:
A. Constantly criticizes my work and rarely has a good thing to say.
B. Is noncommittal about my work and gives me very little feedback.

The worst assignment I can think of is:
A. One that's routine and I've done a million times before.
B. One that has no clear guidelines and for which I've got to create a solution out of whole cloth.

The worst working environment is:
A. One in which there's a lot of politics and people who play the game succeed.
B. One in which only innovation, creativity, people skills, and teamwork are rewarded.

The worst way for my performance to be evaluated would be:
A. Based on seniority, loyalty, and conformity.
B. Based solely on how my work contributed to the company's performance.

The worst thing about work is:
A. When I have nothing to do, and I watch the clock all day.
B. When I have one tight deadline after the next.

The worst trade-off for me would be:
A. If I had to give up job security, in exchange for a chance to make a lot of money.
B. If I had to give up a chance to make a lot of money, in exchange for job security.

The worst corporate culture for me would be one that:
  A. Embraces change and expects people to learn new policies and procedures at the drop of a hat.
  B. Maintains the status quo and tries to keep traditional organizational practices.

Review your responses to get in mind the characteristics you wouldn't want a job to have.

32. MAGNET SKILL

If you've done some of the activities in earlier chapters, you've probably identified a number of marketable skills you possess. The goal here is to find that one skill that outshines all the others. For which skill do you consistently receive praise? What do coworkers, subordinates, and superiors compliment you on? Perhaps it's your ability to manage conflict. Maybe it's the way you come up with great ideas. It could be a traditional skill, such as working well with others or an untraditional one, such as successfully implementing new programs.

Write down your particular magnet skill: _____
_____

Next, consider why we refer to it as a magnet: because there's a natural attraction between your special skill and specific job titles and types of organizations. For instance, a company that is involved in numerous controversies probably would greatly value someone with a crisis management magnet skill; the job title that would line up with this skill might be corporate communications director.

Below, we'd like you to list the job titles and type of businesses or companies that your magnet skill attracts. The odds are that you'll be able to come up with at least three titles and types of businesses for your skill. This should tell you where your application for a job is most likely to be warmly received.

Magnet skill job titles

Magnet skill organizations

33. DRAW YOUR OWN CONCLUSIONS

Do you ever feel uncertain as to what you really want in a job? You may be having second thoughts about your responses to some of the exercises in this chapter, wondering if your stated preferences are accurate. Is money really that important to you? Is it really more important than job satisfaction? These are tough questions, but this activity may help you answer them.

We've used the "paired comparison" format to help you draw some conclusions about the job traits that are really meaningful to you. In the Job Characteristics Survey on the next page, compare the statement in the left column to the one on the right. Then, put a check mark in the box between the two that is closest to the statement that describes your preference.

When you have completed the survey, transfer the total for each column to the spaces provided below:

_____ **A.** guaranteed, consistent income

_____ **B.** higher potential income based on goal achievement

_____ **C.** regular working schedule

_____ **D.** work as many hours as the job requires

_____ **E.** unstructured work, room for creativity/initiative

_____ **F.** structured work, well-defined duties

The numerical totals for each represent trade-offs between different job traits—the higher the score, the more unwilling you'll be to give up that trait. Based on your scores, write your conclusion about what traits you prefer more than others.

Job Characteristics Survey—Part 1

This survey will help identify some fundamental preferences you have for specific job characteristics. This instrument is in a "paired comparison" format. That means you will compare the statement in the left column with the statement in the right column and choose the one that best describes your preference. Put a check in the box between the two items that is closest to the statement that best matches your preference. When you have completed your review of all pairs, total the number of checks in each column. Use the following page to analyze your preferences.

Left statement			Right statement
guaranteed, consistent income	☐	☐	higher potential income based on goal achievement
higher potential income based on goal achievement	☐	☐	regular working schedule
regular working schedule	☐	☐	work as many hours as the job requires
guaranteed, consistent income	☐	☐	regular working schedule
regular working schedule	☐	☐	unstructured work, room for creativity/initiative
unstructured work, room for creativity/initiative	☐	☐	structured work, well-defined duties
guaranteed, consistent income	☐	☐	work as many hours as the job requires
regular working schedule	☐	☐	structured work, well-defined duties
higher potential income based on goal achievement	☐	☐	unstructured work, room for creativity/initiative
guaranteed, consistent income	☐	☐	structured work, well-defined duties
work as many hours as the job requires	☐	☐	structured work, well-defined duties
guaranteed, consistent income	☐	☐	unstructured work, room for creativity/initiative
higher potential income based on goal achievement	☐	☐	structured work, well-defined duties
work as many hours as the job requires	☐	☐	unstructured work, room for creativity/initiative
higher potential income based on goal achievement	☐	☐	work as many hours as the job requires

add the total from each column here ☐ ☐ ☐ ☐ ☐ ☐
A B C D E F

34. REFINING YOUR CHOICES

Sometimes we only possess a general idea of what we want in a career or job. While we might have a good sense of the type of job we'd like, we haven't fully explored all our likes and dislikes related to that job. The subtleties and side issues can often be far more important in total than a particular type of job.

This activity, then, is designed to give you a better understanding of the subtleties and side issues that impact your career choices.

In each of the following ten categories, check in column 1 the statement "a" or "b" that most closely represents your current point of view. If there are any "absolutes" or limits you have, identify them in column 2.

In column 3, review the preferences you identified in each of the ten pairs of items and indicate whether the preference is Critical (C)—you won't consider an organization as a potential employer, unless they meet that criteria; or Desirable (D)—you would like the organization to meet the criteria, but you would not insist on it if other factors suggest they would be a good fit for you.

		1	2	3
Community Involvement	a. I prefer a company that considers itself part of the community. b. It doesn't matter if the organization gives back to the community.			
Controversial Products	a. I would work for a company that manufactured controversial products. b. I wouldn't work for a company that manufactured controversial products.			
Ethics/ Values	a. I can only work for a company that shares my ethics and values system. b. I don't expect the company I work for to have the same values as me.			
Financial Stability	a. I prefer to work for a company with proven financial stability. b. I could work for a company on shaky financial ground.			
History in Business	a. I prefer to work for a company with a rich history in its field. b. I would work for a company just starting out in its field.			
Location of Business	a. I prefer to work for a company in my current geographic location. b. I would willingly move to a new location for the right job.			
Organization Size	a. I prefer working for a small entrepreneurial organization b. The size of the company doesn't matter to me.			
Focus	a. I prefer a company that focuses on profit first and foremost. b. I prefer a company that focuses on customer and employee satisfaction first.			
Religious Affiliation	a. I won't work for a company affiliated with a religion different from my own. b. Religious affiliation of an organization would not matter to me.			
Reputation and Recognition	a. I prefer working for a company that's a known leader in its field. b. A company's name recognition isn't important to me.			

35. THE MATCH GAME

Can you match your work preferences and skills with a specific type of job? While you might not be able to do so off the top of your head, the following step-by-step exercise will facilitate the process.

Step A: Review the other activities from this chapter and write out your:

Top preferences of job traits or work environment
Top skills and personal strengths
Top experiences and training

Step B: List the jobs that best fit your list from Step A. (If you can't do this step yet, skip it and move on to the next step.)

Step C: Get out a pad of paper, a highlighter, and the Sunday paper. Scan the employment ads and highlight the parts of the ads that correspond to the traits and preferences you listed in Step A. (For the moment, don't worry if the actual jobs aren't ones you're interested in.) Now list the job title for each ad you've highlighted part of. Look at the list, which should be long. Cross off any titles that don't interest you, but be open-minded, allowing yourself to consider new possibilities. What jobs have you discovered that you might not have considered before?

Step D: Identify three people who you feel might be able to offer you sound advice about jobs. Pick from among your friends, relatives, mentors, human resource managers, and so on. Show these people your lists from Steps A to C. Ask them to challenge your list and help you expand it further. Given your preferences and traits, what traits would they suggest adding to your list?
Write down their suggestions.

_____

_____

_____

_____

_____

_____

_____

_____

The odds are that you now have at least a few additional jobs that match your requirements.

36. YOUR SURPRISE PACKAGE

You have done a lot of work so far analyzing your skills, experience, training, preferences, and strengths. In the following graphic is a place for you to summarize all this work. Think of all these things as the "package" you bring to an employer. In fact, it is a great package that will be a pleasant gift for an employer to discover. Fill out the blanks as completely as you can, based on the exercises you have completed so far in Chapters 1, 2, 3, and 4.

My Total Package!

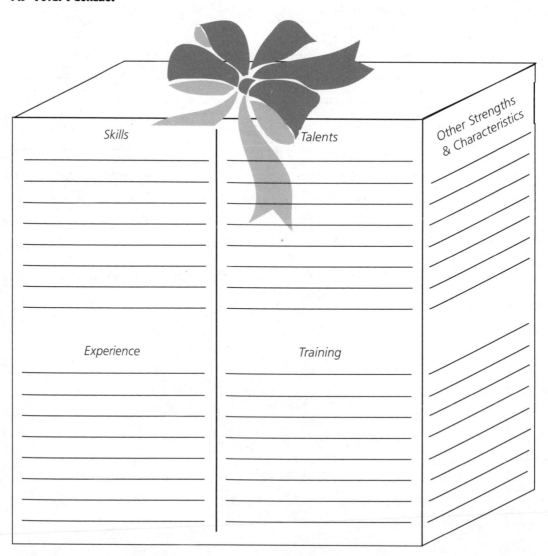

Skills

Talents

Other Strengths & Characteristics

Experience

Training

6

The Best Companies to Work For: Creating Your Personal List

Introduction

We spend too much time during a career search dreaming about working for one particular organization. There are scores of great employers out there for each of us, but we can only find them if we broaden our search.

In this chapter, we're going to give you a number of activities that will help you compile a comprehensive list of potential employers. The following chapter will help you pare down that list, so don't be alarmed if you find yourself with more prospects than you know what to do with.

37. BACK TO THE WANT ADS

Let's start off with something easy. In Chapter 5, you completed Activity 35, The Match Game, that involved reviewing all the want ads published on a given Sunday for skills that fit your package. Now take that set of want ads and write down the names of the companies that placed those ads. Since those ads matched your skill set, it is possible that those employers would be good ones to investigate for positions.

38. BRAINSTORMING INFORMATION SOURCES

Given your initial list of organizations that might make good employers, the logical question is: Do these organizations really suit you? From activities in previous chapters, you've identified jobs that fit with your skills and interests, so you have some sense of what you're looking for. If you love teamwork and are good at it, a company with a team-based structure makes sense for you.

But how do you find out if a company prizes teamwork? For that matter, how do you know if an organization's values match your own?

There are many information sources you can tap to answer these questions. Annual reports, corporate brochures, and articles profiling companies are just three examples. We'd like you to brainstorm some other sources that might prove helpful and list them. If you get stuck, use our list on the following pages.

Review your list. Does it include any or all of the following?

✓ Trade associations
✓ Professional associations
✓ Professional journals
✓ Industry conferences and expositions
✓ Your personal/professional network
✓ Libraries
✓ Your current organization's human resource department
✓ Newspaper articles on the industry or particular companies
✓ Licensing or regulatory agencies

- ✓ State employment security agencies
- ✓ Suppliers to your current employer
- ✓ Former employees of your current employer
- ✓ The Association of Employers
- ✓ College and university placement offices
- ✓ Business publications like *Business Week, Forbes, Fortune, HR Executive, Valueline,* etc.
- ✓ On-line services like Prodigy, America Online, CompuServe, etc.
- ✓ Job fairs

39. ORGANIZATION/JOB TYPE MATCHING

In The Match Game activity in the previous chapter, you created a number of different types of targeted jobs. The exercise here is to list the names of companies that might offer each of those jobs.

Job 1 _____

Employers with those types of jobs:

Job 2 _____

Employers with those types of jobs:

Job 3 _____

Employers with those types of jobs:

Job 4 _____

Employers with those types of jobs:

Job 5 _____

Employers with those types of jobs:

Job 6 _____

Employers with those types of jobs:

Job 7 _____

Employers with those types of jobs:

Job 8 _____

Employers with those types of jobs:

40. MULTIPLY THE POSSIBILITIES

Every organization listed in the previous exercise has numerous competitors, suppliers, marketing services agencies, and other related companies. If you think one of these "relatives" might have a job similar to the one you desire, list the organization in the appropriate space.

Organization 1_____

Competitors or similar organizations are:

The organization's key customers and suppliers are:

Organization 2_____

Competitors or similar organizations are:

The organization's key customers and suppliers are:

Organization 3_____

Competitors or similar organizations are:

The organization's key customers and suppliers are:

These worksheets should get you started on your first three organizations. Please make copies of these worksheets if you need additional ones.

41. DRAW ON YOUR INDUSTRY KNOWLEDGE

Another way to compile a list of relevant organizations is to focus on your particular industry. One of the best resources for this kind of information is the *Business Week Industry Report* or *Corporate Scoreboard* issue. Similar information can be found in *Fortune, Forbes, Barron's Weekly,* or *The Report on Business*, published by the *Toronto Globe & Mail.*

Find a copy of the most recent *Business Week Corporate Scoreboard* issue. Let's say we were looking for companies with plastics products research and design engineers. Now let's say we know that Rubbermaid has some of those kinds of engineers. Find the group of companies that Rubbermaid is in.

Organization: <u>Rubbermaid</u>   Industry Sector: <u>General Manufacturing</u>

Organizations in the same sector:

Let's try it again for Office Depot. This time, keep in mind organizations that may have jobs for retail store managers.

Organization: <u>Office Depot</u>   Industry Sector: <u>Discount & Fashion Retailing</u>

Organizations in the same sector:

Now choose companies you are interested in and find some similar organizations.

Organization: _____ Industry Sector: _____

Organizations in the same sector:

Organization: _____ Industry Sector: _____

Organizations in the same sector:

Organization: _____ Industry Sector: _____

Organizations in the same sector:

Organization: _____ Industry Sector: _____

Organizations in the same sector:

42. INDUSTRIAL ESPIONAGE

It's astonishingly easy to gather critical pieces of information about a prospective employer—far easier than it is for them to gather information about you. The more you know about a company, the better your ability to determine if it's a good company for you. All you need is a little practice using the resources mentioned in this chapter—practice that will come in handy in the next chapter.

If you feel confident about your information-gathering skills, your assignment is to answer the following questions in less than an hour, using whatever resources you wish (skip over the following helpful hints if you want to attempt it on your own).

If you are less confident, give yourself two hours and use the following tools:

✓ *Business Week Industry Report*
✓ Phone calls to shareholder relations departments of relevant organizations
✓ Internet Career Search or company web sites

About Compaq—

1. Where is the organization's headquarters?
2. How many people are employed in the organization?
3. What are the organization's annual sales?
4. What are the primary products and services of the organization?
5. Who is the CEO?
6. Who is the top human resource officer?
7. What is their current stock price?
8. How are their earnings compared to last year?
9. What operations are located closest to your home?
10. What is a phone number to use to reach the company?

About AT&T—

1. Where is the organization's headquarters?
2. How many people are employed in the organization?
3. What are the organization's annual sales?
4. What are the primary products and services of the organization?
5. Who is the CEO?
6. Who is the top human resource officer?
7. What is their current stock price?
8. How are their earnings compared to last year?
9. What operations are located closest to your home?
10. What is a phone number to use to reach the company?

About Ford Motor Company—

1. Where is the organization's headquarters?
2. How many people are employed in the organization?
3. What are the organization's annual sales?
4. What are the primary products and services of the organization?
5. Who is the CEO?
6. Who is the top human resource officer?
7. What is their current stock price?
8. How are their earnings compared to last year?
9. What operations are located closest to your home?
10. What is a phone number to use to reach the company?

Everything You've Always Wanted to Know about Potential Employers ... but Didn't Know Who or What to Ask

Introduction

There's an inherent flaw in the popular "100 Best Companies to Work For" articles. The 100 best for one person might be the 100 worst for another. In the last chapter, you probably compiled a long list of prospective employers. Now the goal is to cut that list down to size.

The more you know about each organization on your list, the easier it will be to cut. The activities here give you a variety of ways to evaluate prospective employers. As useful as these activities are, they're also a lot of fun—who doesn't want to switch roles and critique and reject, rather than be critiqued and rejected?

Let's start out with an exercise that will help you pick and choose from among the organizations you listed in the previous chapter.

43. ARE THESE ORGANIZATIONS RIGHT FOR YOU?

Here is a worksheet to help you analyze the companies you know on the basis of your compatibilities.

Targeting Organizations Matrix

To help you choose specific organizations to pursue further, use the matrix below. In the vertical columns, list the critical criteria you developed in the previous activity. In the horizontal rows, list the organizations you identified in the previous chapter. As you find out information on these organizations, indicate which of your critical criteria each organization meets.

Criteria

Organization

List the organizations that most closely meet your criteria in the spaces below:

1.	
2.	
3.	
4.	
5.	

44. SCAVENGER HUNT

Research doesn't have to be boring, and we think you'll find this game a relatively painless way to get comfortable with looking for suitable employers and information about them. Perhaps you recall the old children's game, Scavenger Hunt, in which children are given a list of objects and told to knock on doors in the neighborhood until they have everything on the list.

The rules of this game are basically the same, only instead of knocking on neighbors' doors, you'll conduct your search through modem, magazine, and other media (see helpful hints at the end of our list for some suggested places to look). Simply take the following list and hunt for the companies that make a match.

Find an organization:

A.   Whose corporate culture sounds ideally suited to your values.

B.   That has announced plans to expand their workforce (or build a facility in the area or open new branch offices).

C.   That has communicated the need to hire people with your set of skills.

D.   That is going through reengineering or other changes that will require people with the skills you possess.

E.   Whose top manager has made statements that make you feel as if the organization would be a great place to work.

F.   That seems to meet three or more of the following job requirements: office location, workstyle (flextime, open environment, etc.), leadership style of CEO, position in industry, size of organization, structure of organization (teams versus hierarchy).

G.   That appears to be "hot," based on articles you've read about them or other information.

H.   That you know people who work for (or have secondhand information about people who work there) and they rave about the organization's attributes.

I.   With an unusual (in your experience) policy or program that dovetails perfectly with your needs (free day care, for instance).

You win the game if you find at least one organization for each of the nine items listed. To help you with your hunt, here are some places you can search for the "items" described on the list:

✓ trade and professional associations
✓ union halls
✓ professional journal listings
✓ conference exhibitors
✓ your network
✓ the library
✓ an organization's marketing or HR department
✓ newspaper and magazine articles about companies
✓ licensing or regulatory agencies
✓ suppliers to the organization
✓ former employees
✓ on-line services, the Internet

45. THE TEN WORST LIST

It's instructive to think about where we wouldn't want to work in a million years. When we think about why we wouldn't want to work in those places, we can search for employers who embody the opposite characteristics. Can you come up with ten companies about which you feel you would rather starve than be their employee? Draw upon your experiences as well as on what you've heard and read. Then compose your list and in a few words describe why you wouldn't want to work there (for instance, organization X—because they treat employees like machines). Keep the list handy for comparison with the companies you find that do seem like prospective employers—there should be a marked contrast between the two lists.

Companies I wouldn't work for in a million years .. and why I wouldn't.

1. _____

2. _____

3. _____

4. _____

5. _____

6. _____

7. _____

8. _____

9. _____

10. _____

46. THE TEN BEST LIST

Now let's take a more positive approach. Exercise 44, Scavenger Hunt, gave you a sense of how you can use various resources to discover names of prospective employers. This time, use those resources in a more free-form style, hunting for companies that seem right for you based on the information you've gained about yourself in this and other chapters. Jot down the names of as many good prospects as you can discover. Then winnow the list down to ten, based on your Values Reality Check (Exercise 2).

Companies I would work for ...

1. _____

2. _____

3. _____

4. _____

5. _____

6. _____

7. _____

8. _____

9. _____

10. _____

47. FINDING INFORMATION NUGGETS

What do you want to know about a potential employer? Well, if you're like most people, you can think of a thousand things. Given limited time, opportunity, and patience to obtain this information, you need to focus on what's really important for you to know. To help you do so, try the following:

✓ Put yourself in the position of an employer about to interview a job candidate. What information would you expect the candidate to know about your organization? Write that information in the space below:

✓ Now think of yourself as someone who wants to invest your hard-earned money in an organization. You're not looking for a tax break; you want an organization that will work for you and that's consistent with your goals and values. What questions would you ask about that organization to know if it's worth your investment?

Write the questions below:

✓ Review the information you generated in the previous two sections. From the lists you generated, develop five questions you believe are most important to ask about a potential employer so you get a feel for who they are and what they do. List those questions on the next page.

1.

2.

3.

4.

5.

✓ Review the list of questions you just wrote. Does your list contain things like:

— the organization's history or service?

— its history in business?

— its reputation in the field?

— the type of customers or market it serves?

— its most recent successes?

— the kind of people it tends to hire?

✓ Review your list one more time. Do you have anything on it about salary, benefits, or promotional opportunities? If so, cross it out. These are issues to consider after you've actually had an interview with the companies in question.

The Point of No Return: What to Do Before Setting Forth on the Interview Path

Introduction

Before attempting to secure an interview at any of your targeted companies, you might want to subject them to a final bit of scrutiny. Getting interviews and going on them requires a significant expenditure of time and energy; you can conserve some of both if you make sure the interviews are really worth the effort.

Look at the activities here as a way to test your interest in a given job at a given organization. If it passes the test, great. If not, don't waste your time on it.

48. SKILL COMPARISON ANALYSIS

By this point, you might have a good idea about the types of jobs you'd like to apply for at the various companies on your list. You may also be aware of the skills those jobs require. If you aren't, make some calls to the human resource departments at those companies, asking about the skills required for the job in which you're interested (most companies have job descriptions that detail these skills).

By doing the skill analysis here, you can determine if you possess the skills a particular job requires (and if you don't, figure out how to get them).

Skill Comparison Analysis

Position Title:			
Skill Required	I Don't Have	I Do Have	Evidence (for skills I have)
Skill Growth (for skills I don't have)		Action Plan (how I can get the skill)	

49. LISTENING TO THE GOSSIP

Sometimes it pays to evaluate a company subjectively, rather than objectively. From your general knowledge about the organizations on your list, you probably have formed an impression of them that's divorced from facts and figures. You've heard various bits of gossip that have led you to form this impression. While gossip can be false, it's often true and therefore is worth at least factoring into the mix. Below we've listed some of the most common rumors, accusations, kudos, and general gossip that circulate around companies. What we'd like you to do is look at this list and place the names of companies after the appropriate piece of gossip.

1. Everyone plays politics there.
2. They're due for a downsizing.
3. You won't find a company that gives its employees a better benefit package.
4. It's the type of company that starts you off with a low salary but really rewards you if you perform well.
5. They work you like a machine.
6. They really are flexible when it comes to individual situations, like working parents or telecommuting.
7. Top management is a boy's club.
8. If you don't golf, you can forget about moving up at that organization.
9. Once you put in your time, it's a country club.
10. It's a great place for nonconformists; if you're able to add value, you can dress as you like and work when you want.
11. They tell you there's only a moderate amount of travel, but you're on the road constantly those first few years.
12. They're going to expand tremendously in the next five years, so there will be a lot of opportunities for people who don't mind working long and hard.

Note that some of these would be considered good and some would be considered bad. The bottom line in considering where you would like to work is which ones would excite you or could you tolerate in the organization you join? If you join an organization whose reputation turns out to be accurate, and you like it—you may have found your long-term employer. However, if you can't tolerate the way they are, you are more likely to be frustrated. This may lead to your being a short-termer with that organization.

50. INSIDE STUFF

Who doesn't want to know in advance what's going to be asked on the test? This activity is designed to prepare you to ask the right questions when you gain an interview with an organization on your top ten list. The information you gleaned from the previous activity is basic stuff; the information you'll get here is inside stuff. What are interviewers thinking about when they're interviewing you? What are they impressed by? What turns them off?

Practicing thinking the way an interviewer thinks can be a valuable exercise. It will enable you to gain insights about the type of questions you should ask during an interview.

Start by role-playing again. You're the interviewer, trying to decide if a candidate is the best one for the job. With that task in mind, answer the following four questions:

What criteria would you use to decide whether to invite the person for an interview in the first place?

What would impress you most/least about a candidate applying for a job?

What would you consider appropriate questions for a job candidate to ask you during the intial interview?

Are there any types of questions or topics the candidate should avoid discussing during this initial interview?

Now that you've come up with your role-playing answers, do a reality check. You can do this by contacting anyone you know who routinely interviews job candidates—someone who works for a search firm or in human resources, or a business owner. Show them how you responded to these four questions and ask them to evaluate your responses. You might also contact the H.R. department of one of your targeted organizations. If you request only a few minutes of their time on the phone, they probably won't mind giving you their take on these four questions.

51. I WILL NOT BE TEMPTED BY ...

Once we enter the interviewing process, we can easily lose our resolve to find a certain type of job. Sometimes we get so sick of the process we'll take anything to end it. Other times we receive offers that are difficult to refuse. The temptations range from high salaries to great perks to prestigious titles. In and of themselves, there's nothing wrong with these temptations. But when they cause us to take jobs we know we should turn down, they're trouble.

Examine the following list of temptations, determine which ones you're particularly vulnerable to, and make a check mark next to them. Keep this list in the pocket of your best interview clothes, so that you can refer to it after you've been tempted to ignore good judgment.

___ The job comes with a corner office, club membership, and free parking.

___ I'll get the title I've always wanted but never had before.

___ The salary is far more than anything I've ever been paid.

___ I'll get to do a lot of traveling to great places.

___ The company's a leader in our industry and well-known throughout the world.

___ The organization has on-site day care, which would really make my life easier.

___ I've always wanted to work for a company that lets its people work flexible hours or from home.

___ The offices are beautiful, the facilities are great and include an on-site health club, and the place looks better than any place I've ever worked.

___ They have a great vacation policy.

___ You can dress however you want.

___ The person who would be my boss actually seems like a reasonable, friendly, kind individual.

___ They offer terrific health benefits.

Remember that the best job will meet many important criteria well—not just one or two of these temptations.

III
SECURING YOUR POSITION

9

How to Build Your Own Network from Scratch

Introduction

The activities in this chapter all revolve around the concept of networking. The odds are that most of you have done some networking at one time or another—at a trade association conference or at a business-related party. But if you're like most people, you've probably missed numerous opportunities to make contacts that might lead to jobs. Here we'll give you a variety of tools and ideas to make and maximize those contacts.

We're going to start you off with a quick quiz that will give you a sense of your networking ability. But the main activity in the chapter will be learning how to "connect" with people you might have thought were impossible to reach.

52. WHAT'S YOUR NIQ (NETWORKING INSTINCT QUOTIENT)?

Are you a naturally good networker? Or do you find it extraordinarily difficult to do things like "work a room"? To find out where you stand, take the following quiz.

1. If you were to overhear someone talking about an interesting job opening that's right up your alley, you would:
   a. Be reluctant to ask for more information unless you knew the person.
   b. Try to overhear what the person was talking about.
   c. Find out the name of the speaker and write a letter suggesting you were interested in the job you overheard the discussion about.
   d. Wait until the conversation ended, introduce yourself, and ask if you could find out more about the job.

2. If an employer indicated that they had no job for you right now, you would:
   a. Thank them for their time and politely exit the interview.
   b. Ask them to keep your resume on file in case anything comes up in the future.
   c. Create a tearful scene, hoping that they'll take pity on you.
   d. Ask them if they know of any other employers with openings for similar positions.

3. If a contact gave you the name of someone who she described as "a good source for a job lead" and you couldn't get past the secretary, you would:
   a. Threaten the secretary with bodily harm if you weren't put through immediately.
   b. Try to sweet talk the secretary.
   c. Give up, deciding the person is probably too busy to help you anyway.
   d. Ask your contact to make a call of introduction for you.

4. You are most likely to network:

    a. At parties.

    b. At business-related functions.

    c. On the telephone.

    d. Anywhere and everywhere.

5. I look for contacts who:

    a. Have the ability to directly offer me a job.

    b. Work for organizations I'd be interested in working for.

    c. Are senior-level people.

    d. Have the potential to hire me, provide me with good career information, or lead me to other valuable contacts.

6. I would guess that I add the following number of names to my business Rolodex each week:

    a. 0

    b. 1-3

    c. 4-6

    d. 7 or more

7. If I were stuck in an elevator in an office building for an hour with ten people I didn't know, I would most likely:

    a. Not talk to anyone.

    b. Talk to one or two people, but I wouldn't learn much about them or what they did for a living.

    c. Talk to a bunch of people, but our conversations wouldn't be of any significance to jobs or careers.

    d. Talk to at least a few people, find out what types of jobs they had, and exchange business cards.

8. If I happened to be introduced to one of the top people in my field at a social gathering, I would:

    a. Barely be able to stammer my name.

    b. Be intimidated and unable to ask relevant questions about possible jobs in the field.

    c. Politely discuss our common area of interest but leave any job search activities for another time and place.

    d. Make sure I at least made my interest in a job known and ask if I could follow up with a letter or phone call soon.

9. If people are going to talk about me when I'm not there, I would:

    a. Want them to embellish my many fine qualities and gifts to humankind.

    b. Prefer they "take the fifth" and not give out any information except my name, rank, and serial number.

    c. Not care what they said, since nothing they said could hurt my job chances.

    d. Prefer to let someone know the facts of my situation, so that they can really know what I can do and perhaps help me out.

The letter "d" is obviously the high NIQ answer for all the questions. If you scored 7 to 9 d's, your NIQ is high; 4 to 6 is average; 0 to 3 is low.

53. IDENTIFYING YOUR NATURAL NETWORK

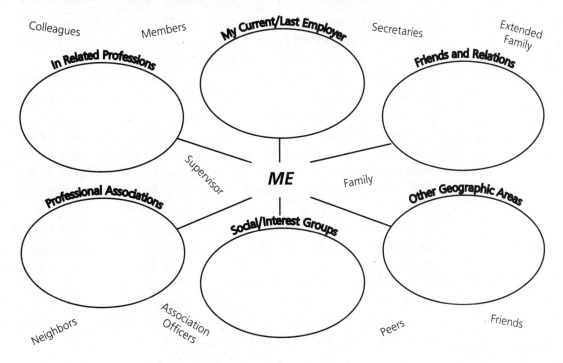

This exercise is designed simply to help you visualize your network. The different circles you move in are represented here, and your task is to fill in those circles with names. Sometimes we don't realize we even have a network until we put it on paper.

54. TARGET NETWORKING

It has been theorized that we can reach anyone in the world through a network of six or fewer people. The remaining activities in this chapter will demonstrate how this is so.

Think of the networking process we're about to introduce you to as a game—a game in which the goal is to make a connection using as few people as possible. Each person needs to be considered a link in the chain of this connection. You are the initiator and the target person is, well, the target. You are doing really well if you can reach the target with three or fewer links. If you can do that with several of the people below *you are connected*! The question you are trying to answer in the following activities is a variation on, "Who is someone who knows someone who knows someone who knows the target?" For demonstration purposes in these activities, we will use Bill Matthews, an author of this book. If you get stuck trying to complete an activity, you'll find some helpful tips using Bill as an example.

Start the process by choosing one of the celebrities from the following list that you do not know.

Troy Aikman, NFL Quarterback

The President of the United States of America

Oprah Winfrey, Talk Show Host

Ross Perot, Perot Systems Corporation

Bill Gates, Microsoft Corporation

Billy Graham, Minister

The Speaker of the House of Representatives

Julia Roberts, Actress

Your city's mayor

Barbra Streisand, Singer

Sandra Day O'Connor, Supreme Court Justice

Nelson Mandela, President of South Africa

Peter Gzowski, CBC Radio

Mario Tremblay, Coach of Montreal Canadians

Gary Trudeau, Cartoonist

Now ask yourself, **"Whom do you know who might know that person?"** Frankly, you might be surprised. Some of our personal acquaintances are very well connected! Think hard! List the people who might know your "celebrity choice" below.

_____

_____

_____

_____

_____

_____

Now check with these folks you've written down and find out if, in fact, they do know the person. There is a pretty good chance of two kinds of base hits. The first one would be a "Yes, I know and have met the person," and your Connections game will be won with one "link." The second kind of base hit would be that your contact knows someone else who knows the person, and you would do very well with only two "links."

Don't be discouraged if you don't make any hits. Just move to the next activity.

55. FIND THE SHARED TRAIT

Investigate your target celebrity as if you were a detective or a reporter working on a profile. This may require some research. You may have to look up articles written about the person, check in *Who's Who*, review association listings. Check with your local librarian or newspaper for ways to find out more.

What organizations are they in?
What associations do they belong to?
What geography do they live or work in?
What is their profession?
What hobbies do they have?
Other characteristics:

In Bill's case he is very active with NASAGA, the North American Simulation and Gaming Association. He likes boats and traveling. He works at Prism Performance Systems in Michigan. He does a lot of consulting, training, and training design. Bill is an author and this book is published by McGraw-Hill, offering two more possible connections. Now it's simply a matter of figuring out the people you know in those organizations, associations, geography, hobbies, etc.

Who do you know who has a similar characteristic to your targeted celebrity? Think about everything from hobbies to professional to charitable interests, and see if you can come up with someone. Then ask your question: Does he or she know Celebrity X? If yes, you've won the Connections game with one "link." Again, it's possible that the person doesn't know the celebrity but does know someone who knows your target, and you win the game with two "links." You may also get a different response—a new idea about where to look for the connection. This could be a referral to another association or group in which the target is known to be involved. If you have no better lead at this time, ask for an introduction to someone in that group. Follow up! This might be your "missing link." You may run dry again. In that case move on to the next activity.

56. MIX YOUR NETWORKS

Most people will have found a two-, three-, or four-link connection to the target celebrity by now. If you haven't, this activity might do the trick. It allows you to stretch your own network to meet the target's network. Remember, the links are there, they are just not visible. If you work hard enough you will find them!

Consider the people in your network who might come in touch with the target's network. What we're really asking you to do is list your network and your target's network and make an educated guess as to where overlaps might occur. Or, to put the activity more precisely, who do you know who can plug you in to the target's network?

Let's take author Bill as an example of how you might go about this. To connect with Bill, you might determine who in your network is aware of NASAGA or might know a member of NASAGA—identifying anyone who has gone through adventure-type training or is a trainer would make sense. They in turn could introduce you to someone who knows about NASAGA; that link can lead you to someone in NASAGA; that next link can help you find someone who knows Bill and would be willing to introduce you to him.

57. TARGET SHIFTING

What if nothing has worked so far? If you've done all the networking exercises up to this point, you've learned enough to take an "end-around" approach.

The process is relatively simple. Choose an alternative target who is linked to your original target. Let's use Troy Aikman as an example. Your alternative should be someone linked with Troy, but also someone with different characteristics—instead of another player, you might focus on a coach or someone in the team's administration. By choosing an alternative target with somewhat different characteristics, you give yourself a fresh chance to connect through a network. All you have to do is restart the networking process, working backwards from your new target. If you can reach this person, you're then just one link away from your original target.

A Flowchart of the Process

Some people have trouble with networking because they become frustrated and stop the process prematurely. Others just lose track of the sometimes complicated series of linkages between people.

To help you avoid these problems, use the following short and long versions of our networking process.

Short Version

Step 1. Determine who we need to meet.

If I don't know them, then—

Step 2. Is there anyone in my network who can introduce me?

If no one knows them, then—

Step 3. What is their network and who do I know who might be in their network?

If no one links me, then—

Step 4. How can I get some links by matching up my network with theirs?

If no one links me, then—

Step 5. Pick a secondary person that definitely knows the person I want to meet and work the process again with meeting them as the goal.

Long Version

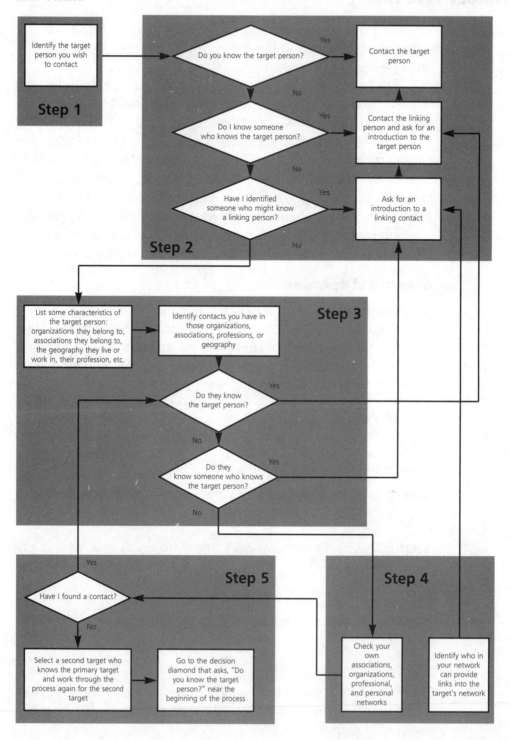

58. CREATE YOUR OWN RUMOR

The final exercise in this chapter is very different from the others. Networking doesn't have to be a labor-intensive activity. You can capitalize on your natural network just by getting the word out that you're looking for a job.

The key is to control that word. If you let people talk about you without putting your two cents in, the odds are that the network will distort who you are and what type of job you want. A casual, negative comment can easily be taken out of context.

How do you get your network to talk about you exactly as the type of job candidate you want to be? Start a rumor about yourself. In the space below, write a few sentences that you want to be on everyone's lips. For example: "John feels he's gone as far as he can go in sales and wants to switch to a supervisory position, and if this company doesn't give it to him, he'll start responding to the headhunters who have been calling him." Don't be shy about making the rumor tantalizing or gossipy, as long as it fits with your career goals.

Obviously you need to use some common sense in creating your rumor—you don't want your boss to be surprised to hear that you're looking for a new job. But you can get people talking about you as a job candidate in informal ways—just give them a nice, juicy rumor to pass around.

Write the career search rumor you want people to talk about below.

_____

_____

_____

_____

_____

_____

_____

_____

59. GETTING THE WORD OUT!

In this exercise take your rumor and turn it into a note to send to some of the people you identified in your network. In the letter you should ask for their help in identifying potential opportunities for you.

Dear

10
Reworking Resumes

Introduction

Resumes are an underutilized tool for job seekers. Too often, people view them as rigid, pro forma documents that contribute only marginally to getting hired. In fact, they can have a significant impact, but only if they're viewed as flexible, creative tools.

This chapter contains activities designed to help you do exactly that. You'll find that you can tinker with your resume in ways you never imagined, and in ways that will make you a much more attractive job candidate.

60. GRADE YOUR RESUME

How does your resume rank on six crucial characteristics? Does it grab the reader's attention immediately or is it dull as dishwater? Does it fail to make clear what type of job you want? Does it send mixed messages about your experience and expertise?

Mark the point on the scale that represents your resume's score for each characteristic, with 1 being the lowest score and 5 the highest. Then add up your scores. 25-30 points—A; 20-24 points—B; 15-19 points—C; 10-14 points—D; 0-9 points—F.

Attention Getting:	I fell asleep reading it.		1 2 3 4 5		I couldn't put it down.
No Contradictions:	"Quality" was spelled wrong.		1 2 3 4 5		Makes perfect sense.
To the Point:	Wanders like Moses in the desert.		1 2 3 4 5		Gets you there in no time flat.
The Experience Adds Up:	Lots of old/unrelated experience.		1 2 3 4 5		Relevant, compelling job history.
It's Clear:	As mud.		1 2 3 4 5		Obvious who I am and what I want to do.
My Edge Shows:	Looks the same as everyone else's.		1 2 3 4 5		One in a million

61. FUN THINGS TO DO WITH RESUMES

Keep the characteristics of a good resume in mind as you go through this activity. Let's start out by trying to choose a candidate for a computer salesperson position—a position that requires an understanding of computers, good relationship-building skills, and excellent communication and demonstration abilities. We have three applicants, each of whom has been asked to submit a mini-resume. Review them and select the best candidate.

SHIRLEY LOUIS

Objective: Computer store position
Experience: Community college computer coordinator. This job required setting up and scheduling computers for students. Applied problem-solving skills to help students achieve their objectives in computer work. Assisted students in selection of software and hardware appropriate for their task.
Other Interests: Studying computer software.

JOE MORELY

Objective: Seeking a position responsible for computer sales.
Experience: Smiths Computer Peripherals. Set up computers with software and hardware accessories for customers.
Other Interests: Public Speaking

FRIEDA WALLS

Objective: Retail sales
Experience: Sales position in Shores Department Store. Worked with customers to identify clothing selections that fit their style and budget. Consistently the top salesperson in my department.
Other Interests: Member National Salesperson Association.

After selecting the candidate that seems best for the position, describe why you made that selection based on the information in the resumes:

_____

_____

_____

_____

_____

_____

Review each resume again. What is the strength of each resume? How would you change each one to make it stronger?

_____

_____

_____

_____

_____

_____

How would a resume look that combines the strengths of all three candidates? Build a resume for Harrison Forth with these combined strengths:

HARRISON FORTH

Objective:

Experience:

Other Interests:

62. TWO RESUMES FOR THE PRICE OF ONE

One resume doesn't always do the job—or get the job. Most of us apply for different types of positions within a general category. As a result, the qualifications we state for Job A aren't necessarily relevant for Job B.

Thus, we need two resumes (and sometimes more). The art of producing two resumes for one person requires a bit of creativity. Take a shot at it in this exercise, where Fred Plain is applying for two different types of jobs: the head mechanic for a local car dealership and the laboratory supervisor for an automobile research facility.

Fred is an action-oriented guy with the requisite experience and education to do both jobs well. He has been the team leader on several research projects in his current position as a research lab technician. He was also the guy everyone went to for solutions when they were stuck on a repair at Joe's Autofixit, where he used to work. Due in no small part to Fred's contributions, Joe's Autofixit was widely acknowledged to be the best repair shop in town, and its reputation has slipped a bit since Fred left.

Fred works hard—10 to 12 hours a day are common—and he's always willing to pitch in and help a co-worker finish a project. He is the vice president of a technician's association, and a report he wrote was published in the national association's newsletter. In terms of his education, Fred was in the vocational studies program at Oakland Community College, and he received straight As in his automotive courses (including an A+ in Laboratory Bench Metrics). In his spare time, Fred helps his buddies with car repairs and can typically be found on weekends in someone's driveway working on a car engine.

Your assignment is to create two mini-resumes for Fred, one for the lab supervisor position and one for the head mechanic job. Use the information provided (as well as additional "facts" about Fred you create yourself) to tailor each resume to the job.

Job/Career Objective:

Contributing Experience:

Contributing Education/Training:

Contributing Associations/Memberships:

Additional Information:

Job/Career Objective:

Contributing Experience:

Contributing Education/Training:

Contributing Associations/Memberships:

Additional Information:

63. PUTTING YOUR BEST PIECE OF PAPER FORWARD— TYPE OF ORGANIZATION

We asked you to customize Fred's resume because he was applying for two different types of jobs. But there are other reasons and ways to customize. You may want to emphasize certain functional skills; you might want to design a resume to appeal to a specific organization; or you may want to write it with a specific reader in mind.

To customize, the key is to identify the characteristics of a particular job, organization, or individual and adjust what's emphasized in your resume accordingly. To practice doing this, try the following exercise.

Five types of organizations are listed below. The first offers a completed example of how you might identify organization characteristics and the resume changes they suggest. Try to complete the list with your ideas about characteristics and changes.

Type of Organization	Organization Characteristics	Possible Resume Changes
Human Services	people-oriented caring low-budget service provider	emphasize relationships demonstrate helpfulness show cost-consciousness
Banking, Financial		
Sales, Customer Service		
High Technology		
Manufacturing		
Other		

64. PUTTING YOUR BEST PIECE OF PAPER FORWARD—ROLE OF INTERVIEWER

Now let's repeat the previous exercise, only this time let's focus on the role of the interviewer. Some interviewers want a lot of technical information about you; others prefer that you focus on "softer" qualities, such as your ability to work with and be tolerant of others. You can make certain assumptions about what will work for a particular interviewer based on his or her job title. While these assumptions aren't always valid, more often than not they will be.

We've listed a number of interviewer roles below. Then we've asked you to identify the interviewer's style type based on those roles and make resume changes based on that style. For our purposes here, choose one of the four interpersonal styles to describe a role: driver, expressive, amiable, or analytic (see Exercise 22 for definitions of each style).

Role of Interviewer	Possible Style Type	Possible Resume Changes
Engineer	Analytic	Include specific data, expand explanations, show applications of problem-solving and analysis
Senior Manager		
Human Resources		
Production Manager		
Finance Manager		
Retail Supervisor		
Other		

65. CUT THROUGH THE CLUTTER

Sometimes your standard resume won't do. It may be that you know you're one of hundreds of applicants for a job, and you have to find a way to make your resume stand out. Or it's possible that you're applying for a job where creativity is critical and your resume should reflect that fact. To help you make your resume distinctive, this activity is filled with thought-starters—a potpourri of ideas to help you separate yourself from the masses.

We'd like to you to run through these ideas—some of which may seem a bit off the wall—and choose at least one that you can implement. *One caution:* Make sure an off-the-wall idea won't bounce into the trash can because it's too wild or weird.

A. The Look

✓ A dash of color—a simple thing with today's color computer printers.

✓ Innovative shape, size, or format—round if you're applying for a job with a tire or record company, oversized if the job requires a lot of hard work, on a computer disk if it's a high-tech job.

✓ Artistic—a drawing or design that relates to your job skills or the job itself.

B. The Style

✓ Humor—a bit of wit that makes the bored resume-reader smile.

✓ Power—a description of your expertise and experience that is more forceful than the norm (i.e., "Raised sales levels 25% despite warnings from superiors that it couldn't be done.")

✓ Poetry—putting resumes or parts of them in verse form.

✓ Biography—turning your resume into a mini-biography that reads better than most resumes. ("The turning point in John Jones' career was when he was promoted to Executive Vice President of the international division.")

C. Substance

✓ Detail—a finely detailed resume that provides the reader with a great deal of pertinent information about your experience and expertise.

✓ Name-dropping—impressing readers by filling the resume with well-known organizations you've worked for, famous business leaders you've worked with, publicity you've received, speeches you've given.

✓ Endorsements—treating the resume as if it were a movie ad or a book and filling it with positive quotes about you from former bosses, mentors, teachers.

✓ Story-telling—including a story from your professional or personal life that illustrates an attribute a prospective employer seeks.

11
Become Your Own Telemarketer

Introduction

It's really not that difficult. After all, you're not asking someone to make a $40,000 purchase (or whatever salary you command) sight unseen. In telemarketing terms, you're offering a no-obligation-to-buy trial offer. Give me an interview, test the merchandise, and see if it's worth keeping.

Research has proven that it takes only 15 phone calls to get two interviews. The activities in this chapter might even increase that number. They're designed to help you feel comfortable and confident when you start making your calls and to help you say the words that will cause a prospective employer to think, "I've got to meet this person."

66. WHAT'S YOUR PDQ (PHONE DIALOGUE QUOTIENT)?

A few lucky souls are natural masters of phone selling. Most of us, however, need to learn and practice various phone techniques. There are certain general rules you should adhere to when you call any company to request an interview. To test how well you know these rules, take the following PDQ test.

1. To convince someone to grant you an interview, you should:
   a. Overstate your qualifications, even if you misrepresent yourself.
   b. Matter-of-factly and modestly express your qualifications, even if you sound somewhat dull.
   c. Express your qualifications in an upbeat manner and in terms of positive accomplishments.

2. If your employer discovers you falsified information about yourself during that initial phone call, the penalty could be:
   a. Life imprisonment (or death by hanging in certain hard-line states).
   b. Termination from the job and civil prosecution.
   c. Nothing; most employers like the spunk and initiative demonstrated by people who stretch the truth to secure interviews.

3. If someone you are trying to meet with says, "Sorry, we have already received as many resumes as we need," your best response is:
   a. "Okay, thanks."
   b. "One more won't hurt."
   c. "I understand you've received a lot of resumes, but I think you'll find my qualifications are a great fit for the position."

4. If you attempt to get an interview and the prospective employer says, "Okay, but I have to tell you that we've already interviewed some great candidates, so you're probably a bit late," you should:
   a. Say thanks for the information and ask the person to call you if another opening comes up.

b. Tell the person that you know some of the people they've interviewed and they're not as great as he thinks.

c. Go to the interview and attempt to make the best impression possible, even if the chances of getting the job are slim.

5. If you can't get through to the person you've been told is the right one to contact to get an interview (and you've left a number of messages), you should:

a. Write a letter or send a fax explaining your frustration at not being able to get through to this person and emphasize your credentials.

b. Keep calling and leaving messages on the assumption that eventually the person will respond.

c. Protest your treatment to the head of human resources and suggest that the company wouldn't have many customers if they treated everyone in such an unresponsive manner.

The right answer to Question 1 is never misrepresent yourself; however, there is nothing wrong with promoting your accomplishments very positively. For question 2, you should know that false information can lead to termination and prosecution. Question 3's response "C" is a great answer to the cliche response, "We have received enough applications already." As to Question 4, always try to get the interview, particularly if you are well qualified for the position, and definitely for the interviewing experience. Question 5 presents a real challenge—faxing your qualifications and interest, and politely expressing the difficulties you've encountered will probably get the best results.

67. THE PERFECT COMEBACK LINE

It's impossible to list all the reasons a prospective employer might supply for not seeing you. Still, we've found that certain ones re-occur with numbing regularity. In this exercise, we'd like you to look at these common rejections and perfect your comeback response. We have provided example comebacks; work to create your own or a variation on ours. The goal is to say the right thing at the right time and turn a rejection into something positive.

In creating comeback lines, remember that your goal is to keep the door open for future opportunities. Think of responses that will lead to referrals or opportunities for other interviews.

"Sorry, the boss is busy right now."

Comeback example: "What time would be better for me to call?"

Your comeback:

"We aren't anticipating hiring anyone for awhile."

Comeback example: "Would it still be possible to talk with you about the type of work in this job?"

Your comeback:

"We're only talking to people with a minimum of five year's of experience."

Comeback example: "My experiences are very significant, enabling me to solve problems that even people with five years in have trouble with."

Your comeback:

"We've received as many resumes as we need."

Comeback example: "My experience makes me an exceptional candidate; are you sure you have enough high-quality candidates?"

Your comeback:

"The position is filled."

Comeback example: "Could you share with me what qualifications the selected candidate had so I better understand how to promote my own qualifications?"

Your comeback:

68. FAVORABLE ODDS

Most people believe that if they start cold-calling companies for interviews, the chances of obtaining one are slim to none. In fact, they're good to great if you make enough calls in the right way. As we've emphasized earlier, research demonstrates that it takes an average of 15 calls to get two interviews and 15 to 20 interviews to receive one or two job offers.

This exercise is your opportunity to test the validity of that research. We'd like you to place 15 calls to the list of companies you've developed in previous chapters (or to any companies of your choosing, if you've jumped straight to this chapter). Take the following three simple steps, and we'll bet that at least one of the 15 calls will lead to a referral, an interview, or a job.

A. When you call, write down the information you receive. The name of the person you talk to, what they tell you about a job opening, what they suggest you should do to follow up—much of this information will be lost if you don't write it down. During a job search, you'll probably make so many calls and talk to so many different people that it will be tough to keep everything straight without a record of your conversation. As a result, potential leads are lost.

B. If you aren't granted an interview, at least get a lead. All you have to do is ask if the contact knows anyone in the industry (or in another part of the company) with a related job opening. Most people don't like turning down your request for an interview, and they'll make an effort to supply you with a lead for another job as compensation.

C. Follow up. Whether you receive an interview or a lead, follow it up with a thank-you letter. A little common courtesy goes a long way, and that letter may be just the thing that differentiates you from all the other people applying for a job.

Organization
Person
Information

Leads?
Organization
Person
Organization
Person
Thank-you sent? ❏Yes ❏Not Yet (schedule a time to write it)

69. ACTIVATE YOUR PITCH

When we get on the phone and make our pitch for an interview, we frequently are self-referential when describing our attributes. We favor descriptions that are limited to who we are rather than what we can do for others. For example:

✓ I am a good worker.

Versus:

✓ I can get the job done for you because I work hard.

The former is a passive way of describing what we can do; the latter is an active statement that clearly communicates a benefit to the prospective employer.

We'd like you to fill in the blanks with some statements you can use during your phone conversations. To do so, focus on how your particular skills can benefit an employer. In phrasing your statement, don't use wishy-washy words like "I hope," "I wish," and "Perhaps." Instead, tell the company how "I can" or "I will" *do* something for them.

A.	Skills I offer that few other candidates will have are …
B.	A valuable contribution I will make is …
C.	Some of my strongest characteristics are …
D.	The experience I bring to your organization is …
E.	The way I will apply _____ to get the job done is …
F.	(Build your own active statement here.)

70. THE 12 THINGS TO DO WHEN YOU'RE ASKING FOR AN INTERVIEW

Does 12 things sound like a lot? It is, especially if you feel tense and rushed as you ask to come in and meet with someone. In the pressured seconds that you have, it's easy to become flustered and forget to obtain an important fact, date, name, or place.

To avoid that problem, here's a 12-point checklist that will help you when you're making your calls.

Request for Job Interview Checklist

1. If you have the name of a person who referred you, start out with that name after your greeting. The person you are talking to will pay closer attention after hearing a familiar name first. (This is not necessary with a switchboard operator, etc.)

2. Repeat your name with your greeting; then listen for the response.

3. Ask for the name of the person in charge of the department, division, or area that you are particularly interested in. Listen for the response. (Note pronunciation and spelling of that person's name.)

4. Ask to speak to that person by name; listen for the response. If you are asked why you are calling, state that you are looking for some information.

5. When you've been connected, call the person by name; listen for a response. Tell the person who referred you (if applicable). Listen for the response; give your name.

6. Give your qualifications. Use power phrases if appropriate. (*Do not* ask for a "job.")

7. Ask for an opportunity to meet and talk. Identify a range of specific days and times to get together. Listen for the response.

8. Repeat your request for a short time to gather information. Listen for a response.

9. Ask for other leads:
   a) Name, company, phone number
   b) Permission to use the person's name

10. Thank the person for the time. Listen for the response.

11. Tell the person you will look forward to your chat or will check back for a more convenient time. Listen for the response.

12. Send a thank-you note.

12

The Interview: Preparing Yourself to Be Grilled and Coming Out Well-Done

Introduction

Some people dread interviews and do poorly in them because of nervousness. Others fail to make a good impression because they're unprepared for questions or because they're unaware of how to present themselves.

Here you'll find activities that will get you ready for any type of job interview. Do you know your interviewing strengths and weaknesses? The toughest questions interviewers are most likely to ask? Or, as the first activity in this chapter explores, do you have the traits most interviewers prize?

71. IF ALL ELSE FAILS—LAST RESORT TACTICS

No matter what you do, you can't break through to the interview stage with a particular organization. People tell you there's a hiring freeze. They say they've already filled the position. They explain that you lack the required experience or expertise. Sometimes you can't even get through to the right person to talk about the position.

If you are desperate, don't give up. Instead, consider some of the following last resort strategies and tactics. We will identify a strategy, you identify the tactics you might use to work that strategy.

Strategy 1—Network to a higher level. Earlier in the book we presented a number of networking tactics; now would be a good time to try them out. What actions could you take to move your inquiries to a higher level?

_____

_____

_____

Strategy 2—Share your feelings. Even though it may not seem like it, the person on the other end of the phone is human, too. Sharing a feeling like, "I am very frustrated that I am not able to communicate my qualifications to the right people. Is there anything else I can do?" might just get to their human side and result in some helpful advice on how to connect better. What action could you take to share your feelings and who would you share them with?

_____

_____

_____

Strategy 3—Make a memorable promise. Tell the person you are calling that you'd be willing to work for free for a two-week trial period; or that you wouldn't take a vacation during the first year of employment; or that you'd arrange a lunch meeting with your former manager to tell them what a great employee you are. The key is to demonstrate how much you want the job. Remember, if you make a promise, keep it, unless it gets renegotiated. What is a promise you might make to become more memorable?

----

72. MAKING THE GRADE ON THE JOB

This worksheet will help you self-evaluate job characteristics.

Making the Grade on the Job

Employers say they are looking for people with specific traits that go beyond just getting the job done. Rate yourself on the following areas:

Self-Evaluation Checklist	Can't make the grade	Need to find a good tutor	Nobody seems to notice	Honor Society material	Top of my class
Demonstrating enthusiasm					
Demonstrating ability & skill					
Demonstrating leadership					
Taking initiative/self-starting					
Taking on responsibility					
Handling change flexibly					
Handling conflict appropriately					
Handling pressure effectively					
Making good decisions					
Getting along with people					
Accepting challenges					
Accepting feedback					
Following directions					
Meeting deadlines					
Working to be the best					

73. 25 QUESTIONS INTERVIEWERS FREQUENTLY ASK

You may know some of the following questions, but you probably have never sat down and thought out your answers to them. The odds are that an interviewer is going to ask at least some of the 25 questions listed here. If you're prepared to answer them, you'll make a solid impression.

This exercise involves writing answers to these questions, but not just any answers. Think about responses that will distinguish you from other job candidates, meet a company's expectations of their employees, and demonstrate your special mix of competencies. Write your responses to the questions on the following pages.

1. Tell me something about yourself.

2. What is your strongest asset? (Give me an example of how you used it.)

3. Why do you want to work here?

4. What do you see yourself doing five years from now? Ten years from now? What are your long-range goals?

5. What jobs have you enjoyed the most? The least?

6. What was your greatest accomplishment in your last position? (Explain.)

7. What kind of relationship did you have with your previous peers?

8. How did previous supervisors treat you?

9. What have you learned from some of the jobs you have held? (Give an example.)

10. What kind of work interests you?

11. What is the ideal job for you?

12. Why did you choose this field of work?

13. Do you prefer working alone or with others? Why?

14. What kind of boss do you prefer?

15. Do you require regular hours?

16. Do you have any problems with working long hours?

17. What does "teamwork" mean to you?

18. What do you consider to be your greatest strengths and weaknesses? (Give work-related examples.)

19. What criteria are you using to evaluate the department for which you hope to work?

20. What have you done that shows initiative and willingness to work? (Give an example.)

21. What interests you about our departments, products, or services?

22. Why do you think you might like to work for our department?

23. Why do you think you would enjoy this particular job?

24. What special qualifications do you have for this job?

25. What did you dislike about your previous job?

74. KNOWING YOUR INTERVIEWER

It is useful to know the interpersonal style of your interviewer. In Chapter 4, you completed a short interpersonal style instrument from International Learning, Inc. In this exercise, you will think about ways to most effectively communicate with people displaying the different styles.

Obviously, interviewers can be any one of the style types described in Chapter 4. In general you could think of Drivers as strictly business. Amiables are friendly and comfortable to talk with. Analytics will want to spend time on the details backing up your qualifications. Expressives may very well talk more than you do in an interview. While it's true that there are many interviewers who don't fall neatly into any of these categories, there are others who fit perfectly. Below are some statements or questions that an interviewer might make. Since this exercise is about thinking through what the style of the interviewer might be, identify the most likely style indicated by the statement or question and consider how to best adapt your interviewee style to that style. (Now might be a good time to review the Chapter 4 information on interpersonal styles.)

Remember, the four styles to select from are: Driver, Amiable, Analytic, and Expressive.

A. Tell me about the work you performed on your last job.

Possible style:

Ideas on how to communicate in the interview:

B. Oh, you worked at the National Bank, too? I was there for three years in the human resource department. I really liked the people there. How did you find working there?

Possible style:

Ideas on how to communicate in the interview:

C. We are really excited about our teams and the people on them. They do great work together and the people seem to really enjoy being on them. We conduct training for them and get them skilled to do their jobs and operate as team members. Our policies are oriented to reinforce teamwork too. Even our profit-sharing plan is. We have one of the best profit-sharing plans and our 401(k) is very good, too. Have you ever been on a business team?

Possible style:
Ideas on how to communicate in the interview:

D. Your resume indicates that you were with ABC Engineering as a technician from 1988 to 1992. Tell me about your responsibilities there and your key accomplishments. I would also like to know of any particular performance measures they used that applied to your work as a technician.

Possible style:
Ideas on how to communicate in the interview:

Consider that, even if we are interviewing with different people for the same job, the way we interview might be very different. If we adapt our behaviors to others' styles, we have a better chance to build a good relationship with them, increasing our chances for an offer. With Drivers, work to be direct and to the point. With Amiables, discuss relationships and activities or experiences from a people-oriented viewpoint. With Expressives, be prepared to listen a lot. With Analytics, be prepared to share data and information that supports your qualifications.

75. EXTRA CREDIT QUESTIONS

If you think the questions in the previous exercise were tough, wait until you get a look at these stomach-churners. These are the ones that you wish weren't asked, that have you searching desperately for a cogent response. Instead of searching desperately, just think about and answer the following questions in advance:

✓ Why should we hire you?

_____

_____

_____

✓ What makes you the most qualified person for this job?

_____

_____

_____

✓ Why did you (do you want to) leave your last (current) job?

_____

_____

_____

✓ What is the worst thing your last supervisor would say about you?

_____

_____

_____

✓ Give an example of how you handled a pressure situation in your last position.

_____

_____

_____

✓ Give an example of how you handled a conflict with a boss or supervisor in your career.

_____

_____

_____

✓ How would you handle it if you noticed someone was:
—falsifying expense reports?

_____

_____

_____

—making false promises to a customer?

_____

_____

_____

—using company stamps for personal mail without paying for them?

_____

_____

_____

—stealing from someone else's locker or desk?

_____

_____

_____

✓ Are you willing to relocate/travel?

_____

_____

_____

✓ What salary do you expect?

_____

_____

_____

76. INTERVIEWING WITH STYLE

Few people like to see themselves on film or video. Yet, as uncomfortable as it may seem, it can be very beneficial to practice your interview skills on tape and review them. Find someone to serve as your interviewer. Ask them to play the part realistically and ask you questions an actual interviewer may ask. (They can choose from the lists of questions presented in earlier activities in this chapter.)

Focus the camera directly on you, the interviewee. Record an interview of at least a half-hour. When finished, review the tape. Each of you should complete the worksheet below independently. When you have both completed your worksheets, compare notes.

If you don't have access to a videotape recorder, you and your interviewer can still complete the performance and take notes.

Interview Criteria	Fine Job	Good Work	Needs Work	Comments
Maintains appropriate eye contact				
Speaks clearly—tone, tempo, volume				
Uses correct language/no jargon				
Provides directs answers to questions				
Provides examples where appropriate				
Displays openness and enthusiasm				
Demonstrates knowledge of organization				
Demonstrates knowledge of job				
"Sells" oneself as the best candidate				
Leaves positive lasting impression				

77. KNOWLEDGE IS POWER

Knowledge is power! In previous chapters we showed you where you can go to find out information on potential employers to decide whether or not they would fit into your list of targeted organizations. Those same resources and others can again be utilized as you prepare for actual interviews.

Potential employers want to know that you have some understanding of the issues and trends that face them and others in their industry. They are usually favorably impressed with candidates who demonstrate insight into the key problems and challenges a company faces. In this activity, you will be going on another information hunt. As you identify companies you intend to interview with, complete the worksheet on the following page based on your review of appropriate resources, including those mentioned in previous chapters, trade publications, informational interviews with competitors, and discussions with members of your career search network.

Organization name:
C.E.O./President:
Industry:
Major industry concerns and trends:
Major products/services:
Major competitors:
Major company concerns and trends:
Other pertinent information:

13
How Did the Interview Go?

Introduction

Having interviewed many people over the years—and having worked with many others who conduct interviews—we can tell you that the people who perform best are those who have done their homework about prospective employers. They don't ask, "How can I make a contribution to your organization?" Instead, they've researched the company and know how they can make a contribution. During the interview, they communicate that fact convincingly.

Great interviewees know their strengths and weaknesses; they're honest and open to suggestions; and they're articulate about how they can help prospective employers meet their objectives.

Does this sound like you? Think about how you've felt after an interview. If you've felt as if there was at least some room for improvement, the activities in this chapter are for you. We'll begin with three exercises built around the three "phases" of most interviews.

78. INSTANT REPLAY: KEEPING A WHAT/HOW "TAPE" OF THE ACTION

What happened in your interview? If you don't write it down in an organized fashion shortly after your meeting, you're likely to forget some things and distort others. This exercise will facilitate keeping what took place straight.

In doing this exercise, think about your interview as three distinct phases: Introductions (the get-to-know-you part), Sharing Your Credentials (when you discussed your background and interests) and Exploring the Employer (when you asked the questions and obtained information about the job).

The Introductions phase of the interview begins when you show up at the waiting room and ends with the first question about your background. In this phase the interviewer and interviewee get warmed up, they socialize, before getting to the business of the interview. This phase is probably more important than you think; more than one interviewer has been turned off by a job candidate's demeanor. Remember, first impressions count.

The Sharing Your Credentials phase starts with that first question about your background and ends with the interviewer asking what you would like to know about the company. This is probably the most important part of the interview. This is your chance to point out why you are the most qualified and interested candidate for a position.

In Exploring the Employer, you ask questions about the company. Here's when you ask constructive questions that demonstrate your interest in helping the organization meet objectives.

Write down, as best as you can recall, what happened in each phase of the interview. List questions that were asked, your responses, and any other elements you can recall. Complete the worksheets on the next three pages.

Introductions

What happened?

How I felt:

How the interviewer appeared:

Sharing Your Credentials:

What happened?

How I felt:

How the interviewer appeared:

Exploring the Employer:

What happened?

How I felt:

How the interviewer appeared:

79. SELF-ANALYSIS

Now you need to analyze your performance. Remember each part of the interview. Consider how you performed in each phase. Were you able to make yourself and the interviewer comfortable? How did you respond to questions the interviewer asked? How well did you do asking questions? Complete the worksheets below and on the next two pages.

Introductions

What went well?

What could have been better?

Things I will do differently next time:

What went well?

What could have been better?

Things I will do differently next time:

What went well?

What could have been better?

Things I will do differently next time:

80. TURN BACK THE CLOCK

Here's your opportunity to rewrite history—well, at least to rewrite the interview script. This exercise will help you determine how to answer the questions when they come up in the next interview. Imagine you are able to turn the clock back and have a second chance at answering the interviewer's questions. Write exactly what you would say to answer the questions that were asked. Don't forget to identify the questions you wish you had asked of the employer.

What specifically would you say differently in the next interview? Complete the following worksheet.

Introductions:

Sharing Your Credentials:

Exploring the Employer:

81. KNOW THY EMPLOYER

Take a moment to identify what you have learned about the prospective employer from your interview. Then list what you don't know because you didn't ask.

What I learned:

What I wish I'd asked:

If you're like most people, you didn't ask a lot. We've found that many interviewees are so concerned about making a good impression and answering the interviewer's questions that they fail to learn anything new about a given company. The following will help you avoid making that mistake again.

Did you identify any of the following questions? Circle any questions on this list that would be appropriate to ask in your situation.

- ✓ What are the organization's plans for the future?
- ✓ What kind of work schedules do you keep?
- ✓ What are the career path possibilities for this position?
- ✓ How does the performance evaluation process work?
- ✓ What factors are most important for good performance evaluations?
- ✓ How can I learn more about the benefit programs?
- ✓ What are the key areas of performance that contribute to organization success?
- ✓ What are the particular goals or objectives of this department?
- ✓ How do you handle overtime work scheduling?
- ✓ Can you describe the work environment and work style?
- ✓ What is the best way to get up to speed on the job quickly?
- ✓ How can I best make a contribution while learning the job?
- ✓ What are the expectations for travel on the job?
- ✓ What tools or equipment are employees expected to provide? Are they insured by the company?
- ✓ What is the dress code for people working in this area?
- ✓ What kind of training does the company provide? Any kind of tuition assistance?
- ✓ What additional information would help you understand my qualifications for the job?
- ✓ What should our next steps be?

82. THE INTERVIEWEE REPORT CARD

Grade yourself on the following interview performance categories. Use the following scale and fill in the blank to the left of each item with your self-determined grade.

A Headed for the interviewee hall of fame.

B Should definitely get a hall pass.

C Headed back to study hall.

D Might end up out in the hall.

E Did you say hall of shame?

_____ I was on time and properly groomed.

_____ I was prepared with knowledge of the position and the organization.

_____ I was relaxed and friendly.

_____ I presented my credentials effectively and didn't get flustered by any tough questions.

_____ I asked constructive questions that gave me good information and painted a good picture of my interest in the job.

_____ We closed the interview with next steps that will improve my odds of winning the job.

83. WHAT'S WRONG WITH THIS INTERVIEW?

Here's an amusing activity that will also enable you to test what you've learned from this chapter. Instead of focusing on your own interview performance, let's take a look at how Diana Cirrus did. Diana was applying for an assistant executive director position with a large not-for-profit association. During the interview with the association's executive director, Diana made a number of mistakes. Your challenge is to identify the ten mistakes she made, underlining them and listing them in the space provided at the end of the exercise. Make sure you explain what each mistake was. The following is a written "video" of Diana's interview with Marjorie Clammer.

> Diana arrived right on time for her interview with Marjorie Clammer. Marjorie's secretary led Diana into the office, where Diana and Marjorie shook hands.
> "Glad to meet you," Marjorie said.
> "Glad to meet you, too, Ms. Clammer," Diana replied.
> "Please, call me Marjorie."
> They sat down and Marjorie began talking about the terrible weather and hoping that Diana didn't have any problems getting to the association's office. Diana said it was lucky that she left early, adding that she assumed that the association was flexible with its starting time, since it really was located in an inconvenient suburban location for people who lived in the city.
> "Most of our people live out here," Marjorie explained. "Maybe that's something you should consider, if you get the job."
> "Oh, I don't know. I'm really a city person, and I've found that I don't have much in common with suburbanites."
> Marjorie began asking Diana about her credentials for the position. In response to Marjorie's query about Diana's experience supervising others, Diana told one of her favorite anecdotes about how she had been thrust into her first supervisory job when her boss suddenly quit and she found herself in charge of 25 people, most of whom resented her at first, resulting in a number of now-amusing conflicts.

The story took about five minutes to tell, and when she was done Marjorie asked her to identify her strength as a supervisor.

"To be honest with you, Ms. Clammer, it's my ability to work with anyone, regardless of their race, sex, or background."

"But," Marjorie responded, "on your job application form you wrote that you left your last employer because you couldn't get along with your superior."

"Oh, that. Well, no one could get along with Donald Watson, he was such an overbearing jerk."

Marjorie then questioned her about any weaknesses.

"I don't consider this anything major, but I really am not a morning person. As the day goes on, I really become sharper. To me, an ideal work schedule would be 11 to 7."

When Marjorie asked if Diana had any questions about the company, Diana began relating that one of her strengths she'd forgotten to mention was her organizational ability, emphasizing that she was a very structured, logical person.

"You know," Diana asked, "one thing I'm curious about is the atmosphere here."

"What do you mean?"

"Well, the last place I worked there was so much pressure on everyone, no one could do a good job. Everyone was looking over their shoulder and scared of making a mistake."

Marjorie explained that because the association was not-for-profit, there was probably a bit less pressure than in a for-profit enterprise.

"That's good," Diana said, "though it's too bad that not-for-profits don't pay as well as corporations."

As Diana was leaving the office, she smacked herself on the forehead and said, "I almost forgot. I wanted to tell you that I have a vacation planned for early next month, so if I get the job, I'm going to need at least a few days off then, and of course I'll understand if they're not paid days, but I'm not going to be able to get a refund, so I really have to go."

Now go back to the story, underline the mistakes you find and explain the mistakes here:

1. _____

2. _____

3. _____

4. _____

5. _____

6. _____

7. _____

8. _____

9. _____

10. _____

Diana arrived right on time for her interview with Marjorie Clammer. Marjorie's secretary led Diana into the office, where Diana and Marjorie shook hands.

"Glad to meet you," Marjorie said.

"Glad to meet you, too, Ms. Clammer," Diana replied.

"Please, call me Marjorie."

They sat down and Marjorie began talking about the terrible weather and hoping that Diana didn't have any problems getting to the association's office. Diana said it was lucky that she left early, <u>adding that she assumed that the association was flexible with its starting time, since it really was located in an inconvenient suburban location for people who lived in the city.</u> ①

"Most of our people live out here," Marjorie explained. "Maybe that's something you should consider, if you get the job."

<u>"Oh, I don't know. I'm really a city person, and I've found that I don't have much in common with suburbanites."</u> ②

Marjorie began asking Diana about her credentials for the position. In response to Marjorie's query about Diana's experience supervising others, Diana told one of her favorite anecdotes about how she had been thrust into her first supervisory job when her boss suddenly quit and she found herself in charge of 25 people, most of whom resented her at first, resulting in a number of now-amusing conflicts.

<u>The story took about five minutes to tell,</u> ③and when she was done Marjorie asked her to identify her strength as a supervisor.

<u>"To be honest with you, Ms. Clammer, it's my ability to work with anyone, regardless of their race, sex, or background."</u> ④

"But," Marjorie responded, "on your job application form you wrote that you left your last employer because you couldn't get along with your superior."

"Oh, that. <u>Well, no one could get along with Donald Watson, he was such an overbearing jerk."</u> ⑤

Marjorie then questioned her about any weaknesses.

"I don't consider this anything major, but I really am not a morning person. As the day goes on, I really become sharper. To me, an ideal work schedule would be 11 to 7." ⑥

When Marjorie asked if Diana had any questions about the company, Diana began relating that one of her strengths she'd forgotten to mention was her organizational ability, emphasizing that she was a very structured, logical person. ⑦

"You know," Diana asked, "one thing I'm curious about is the atmosphere here."

"What do you mean?"

"Well, the last place I worked there was so much pressure on everyone, no one could do a good job. Everyone was looking over their shoulder and scared of making a mistake." ⑧

Marjorie explained that because the association was not-for-profit, there was probably a bit less pressure than in a for-profit enterprise.

"That's good," Diana said, "though it's too bad that not-for-profits don't pay as well as corporations." ⑨

As Diana was leaving the office, she smacked herself on the forehead and said, "I almost forgot. I wanted to tell you that I have a vacation planned for early next month, so if I get the job, I'm going to need at least a few days off then, and of course I'll understand if they're not paid days, but I'm not going to be able to get a refund, so I really have to go." ⑩

1. Starts out the interview with a complaint.
2. Insults most of association's employees, possibly including Marjorie.
3. Tells long-winded story, wasting precious interview time.
4. Contradicts what she wrote on job application form.
5. Not only demonstrates her inability to get along with a superior, but names him—two mistakes in one.
6. Names her ideal work schedule, which is not the work schedule of the association.
7. Another double mistake—not only responds inappropriately to Marjorie but contradicts herself by saying she's an organized person by answering a question in a disorganized manner.

8. Suggests to Marjorie that she won't do well when faced with the deadlines that are part of any job.

9. Demonstrates resentment of low pay of not-for-profits.

10. Double mistake—ends the interview on a sour note and also makes a demand on Marjorie before she even has the job.

14
Responding to the Offer ...
or the Lack of One

Introduction

Is it an offer you can't refuse or one you should refuse? What should you do during that agonizing period between the interview and hearing from a prospective employer? These and other post-interview questions can be difficult ones to answer, and it's easy to think all your work is done once the job interview has been completed.

In this chapter, we'd like to offer you some exercises that will help you avoid mistakes and capitalize on opportunities that are common to the post-interview period. Let's start with a quiz to help evaluate your instincts in this area.

84. POST-INTERVIEW PUZZLERS

The following questions give you the opportunity to test the likelihood of making the right or wrong moves after the interview.

1. When you haven't heard from the prospective employer three days after the time the interviewer said you would hear, you should:
   a. Call the interviewer to say politely, but firmly, that you'd expected to hear something before now.
   b. Figure you won't get the job and accept another one, even if it's not as good as the one you were waiting for.
   c. Call the interviewer and mention a particular attribute you have in order to strengthen your case.
   d. Drop the interviewer a thank-you note, mentioning how much you enjoyed the interview and are looking forward to hearing about the job.

2. If you receive more than one offer, you should:
   a. Take the highest one.
   b. Tell each prospective employer that you've had another offer and that you want them to bid for your services, using salary and other perks.
   c. Decide based on the criteria you've established for the best possible job, even if it means accepting the lower-salary offer.
   d. Reject them if they're not perfect offers, since you're obviously an attractive job candidate who will receive other offers.

3. After you receive and accept an offer, you should respond to those who helped you with your job search by:
   a. Not bothering them with additional calls or letters—they've probably already forgotten that they helped you.
   b. Just thanking those who really gave you useful leads; it would take forever to thank everyone you talked with on the phone.
   c. Thanking everyone who helped you by phone or letter.

d. Taking them out to lunch or dinner, telling them you're in their debt and that if ever they need a favor, you promise you'll help them out.

4. If you don't receive any job offers, you should:
   a. Ignore the rejections; if you believe in yourself, you shouldn't concern yourself with others who don't.

   b. Do everything possible to discover why you didn't receive an offer in order to correct any possible flaws in your approach.

   c. Consider looking at opportunities in a new, unrelated field, since you're ill-suited to your current field.

   d. Keep applying for jobs at the companies that rejected you; these companies will eventually learn to admire your persistence and hire you.

Answers

1. **d.** A thank-you note is a good follow-up when you haven't heard from a company; it's a polite, appreciated way to remind the company that you're out there waiting to hear from them.

2. **c.** Your criteria for the best possible job should guide you in this pleasant situation. While salary should be one of your key considerations, it should not be the only one.

3. **c.** Thanking everyone is wise, not only to be courteous, but to keep your network alive and well for the next time you're looking for a job.

4. **b.** It's almost worth not getting a job if you can learn the reasons why you didn't get it. A forthcoming interviewer can provide you with invaluable information about weaknesses in your resume, interviewing style, background, and so on—weaknesses that you can usually eliminate.

85. MAGIC FORMULA

If you're like most people, you've probably received a job offer and agonized over whether to accept it. You find some aspects of the offer to your liking, while other aspects turn you off. Part of you wants to take it and part of you wonders if you should turn it down in anticipation of better offers. If only there were some magic formula to decide matters.

Well, the following might not strictly qualify as magic, but it does give you a formula with which you can evaluate an offer.

Start by referring to the matrix you created in Chapter 7 in the Targeting Organizations Matrix (Activity 43). Use it to list your criteria for a desirable job. Write them at the top row of the blank worksheet.

Next, review these criteria and determine which is the single most important one right now. This criterion becomes the benchmark against which you'll compare your other criteria. Before moving forward, take a look at the example worksheet on page 187.

Now, we'd like you to assign a numerical value to each criterion. Your key criterion (your most important criterion) automatically receives a value of 5; the others should range between 1 and 5 (the latter number can be used if there're more than one criterion that're key) based on their importance to you. On the worksheet, enter the number value for each criterion on the first row of the worksheet, under the criterion.

Next, list the organizations with whom you've interviewed and from whom you might receive (or already have received) an offer. Write these in the far left-hand column.

Look at the "Criteria Match" guide at the bottom of the worksheet and enter the number appropriate to each organization for each criterion. For instance, if a given criterion is a perfect match with what the best organization on this criterion is offering, enter 5; if it's far from a match, enter 1. Write each criterion match score in the criterion match row under the respective criteria.

Now multiply the Criteria Value number for each criterion by the Critical Match number for each organization (if you would like help, look at the sample worksheet). Write this down in the weighted score row following each organization name. Then, calculate the total score for each organization by adding weighted scores across the row.

While you shouldn't simply decide "high score wins," you can use the scores as a good guide for your decision making about job offers from each of your listed organizations. This is a great tool if you're weighing more than one offer and if there's nothing on the surface to help you choose one over the other.

Sample Worksheet

Criteria Hurdle Example

Criteria		Challenging Work	Benefit Package	Flexible Hours	Reasonable Commute <20 miles	Advancement Opportunities	No Travel Required	Totals
	Criteria Value	5	5	3	3	4	2	
Mc Burgerland	Criteria match	3	4	2	5	1	5	
	Weighted score	15	20	6	15	4	10	70
Toyzntots	Criteria match	3	2	5	4	3	5	
	Weighted score	15	10	15	12	12	10	74
ShopRDrop	Criteria match	4	1	3	4	4	4	
	Weighted score	20	5	9	12	16	8	70

Criteria Values

5 = Critical to my survival
4 = Hard to live without it
3 = Definitely a tie breaker
2 = I'd probably survive without it
1 = I'll never miss it if it's not there

Criteria Match

5 = Perfect match!
4 = More than enough to suit me
3 = About halfway there
2 = Who are you trying to kid?
1 = Pitiful, just pitiful!

Criteria Hurdle Example

Criteria								Totals
Criteria Value		5	5	3	3	4	2	
	Criteria match							
	Weighted score							
	Criteria match							
	Weighted score							
	Criteria match							
	Weighted score							
	Criteria match							
	Weighted score							
	Criteria match							
	Weighted score							
	Criteria match							
	Weighted score							
	Criteria match							
	Weighted score							
	Criteria match							
	Weighted score							
	Criteria match							
	Weighted score							

Criteria Values

5 = Critical to my survival
4 = Hard to live without it
3 = Definitely a tie breaker
2 = I'd probably survive without it
1 = I'll never miss it if it's not there

Criteria Match

5 = Perfect match!
4 = More than enough to suit me
3 = About halfway there
2 = Who are you trying to kid?
1 = Pitiful, just pitiful!

86. SEVEN QUESTIONS TO ASK BEFORE ACCEPTING ANY OFFER

Basically, these questions force you to determine what you believe you'll like about the job and the problems that you foresee. Better to answer these questions now rather than later.

1. What is the best part about the position you've been offered?
2. What will be the most fun part of the job?
3. What parts of the job will you appreciate most?
4. What people at the company seem like they'll be interesting and fun to work with?
5. What problems do you anticipate with the job?
6. Can you handle these problems?
7. How will you handle these problems or adapt to the problematic situations they produce?

If you found that you had trouble supplying responses for the first four questions, that may be a sign that this job is wrong for you.

87. NEGOTIATING BY THE NUMBERS

There are all sorts of theories about how to negotiate. The tool we're presenting here is based on the theory that everything is negotiable and trade-offs are the best negotiating strategy. While it's fine to ask for a larger salary than offered, you may find that your prospective employer refuses to give you what you want. In that case, you might want to use some trade-offs.

Start by evaluating the specifics of an offer based on the following elements:

✓ Salary
✓ Vacation time
✓ Health insurance
✓ Retirement (or other savings) plan
✓ Stock options
✓ Bonuses (policies/expectations)
✓ Work hours
✓ Working conditions (safety, amount of travel, deadline pressure, etc.)
✓ Perks (parking, day care, company car, etc.)
✓ Other

Rate each listed element of the offer on a scale of 1 to 10, with 5 signifying an acceptable level (below 5 is unacceptable, above 5 is more than acceptable).

Look over the scores for each element and determine where there's room to negotiate. For instance, if the salary receives a 9 but the vacation time receives a 2, you may want to suggest taking a bit less salary (moving it from a 9 to an 8) in exchange for more vacation time (moving it from a 2 to a 5).

List three trade-offs of this type you'd be willing to make and negotiate your offer accordingly:

Trade-off #1:
Trade-off #2:
Trade-off #3:

88. IF YOU STILL CAN'T DECIDE

Sometimes it seems impossible to decide about an offer. For every positive, there's a negative. Part of you says, "Take it, you might not get another offer for months or years." Part of you says, "Don't take it; you'll regret you did from the day you start working."

This exercise functions as a tiebreaker. An earlier exercise helped you evaluate an offer based on your criteria for the best possible job. If you're still on the fence, then consider these two issues: (A) Frustration and (B) Future Goals. A bad reason for taking a job is because you're frustrated with the search process and just want to end the darn thing. A good reason for taking it is that the job will help you achieve your future goals. See how you answer the following questions in these two areas and if your answers push you toward or away from the offer.

A. Frustration

✓ How long have you been out of work?

✓ Which word best characterizes your feelings about the job search process? Challenging; Ambivalent; Unpleasant; Agonizing.

✓ During the process, did you feel as if you were never going to receive a job offer?

✓ Do you feel as if you've used up all your job leads?

✓ Are you under serious financial pressure to find a job quickly?

B. Future Goals

✓ What kind of job would you like to be doing in five years? What are some characteristics of that job? What kind of background and skills are required by that job?

✓ Does the current offer seem like a good match for this type of future job?

✓ How will the current offer help you achieve this future job goal?

✓ What parts of the job(s) being offered will prepare you for your future work?

89. REBOUNDING FROM REJECTION

You didn't get the offer. Naturally, you're disappointed. But you shouldn't get stuck. Fretting for days, weeks, or months over not being hired won't help you the next time a job opportunity appears. Analyzing why you were rejected and taking steps to address the problem will help you. The three-step analysis/action plan should enable you to learn from your rejections.

Reasons for Rejection

A. The following are the most common reasons people lose out on jobs. If you're sure why you were rejected, make a check mark next to the appropriate reason (or reasons). If you're not sure, ask your interviewer—you might even want to fax this list and have the interviewer check the reasons.

✓ Poor personal appearance

✓ Sloppy preparation of job application

✓ Late arrival for interview

✓ Poor eye contact with interviewer

✓ No or poor work record

✓ Discussion of personal problems

✓ Not willing to start at bottom

✓ Overbearing and overaggressive

✓ Inability to express oneself clearly

✓ Lack of planning for career—no goals

✓ Lack of confidence—nervous

✓ Failure to ask questions about job

✓ Overemphasis on money—interested only in dollar offer

✓ Poor scholastic record

✓ Makes excuses relative to unfavorable factors in record

✓ Lack of tact

✓ Lack of maturity

✓ Lack of courtesy

✓ Criticism of past employers/bosses

✓ Marked dislike for schoolwork

- ✓ Lack of vitality
- ✓ Merely shopping around
- ✓ Wants a job only for a temporary period
- ✓ Lack of knowledge of field of specialization
- ✓ No interest in company or in industry
- ✓ Emphasis on "who I know"
- ✓ Cynical
- ✓ Indication of strong prejudices
- ✓ Indefinite response to questions
- ✓ Unwilling to consider relocation
- ✓ No interest in community activities
- ✓ Other _____

B. Was the reason you were rejected something you can control? In other words, can you take some action (acting differently in interviews, developing a skill, etc.) that would eliminate the rejection reason?

_____

_____

_____

C. If you answered "yes" to B, write down the specific things you will do to avoid being rejected for the same reason.

_____

_____

_____

90. TURNING REJECTION INTO ACCEPTANCE

Sometimes rejection is a misnomer. An organization may interview 100 candidates for a job, and you're #2 on the list. That doesn't make you any more employed than #100, but it does mean that you were rated highly and positively by the organization. In many instances, companies let runners-up know how well they did and that they came close to getting the job. Rather than be disappointed and frustrated when this happens, use it to your advantage by taking the following steps in the wake of your rejection:

✓ Send a thank-you letter to all the people with whom you interviewed, making a point of saying that you haven't given up hope of still landing a job with the organization and hope they won't give up either.

✓ About a month after being rejected, call the interviewer and arrange to go out to lunch or just for some time to get together. Explain that you were impressed at the interview and would appreciate answers to a number of questions you have about your job search. During the meeting, you certainly should talk about your search, but also explore other openings at the organization and get the names of others you might contact.

✓ Write to the people on your list, emphasizing how close you came to getting a job with their organization and how you hope they'll tell you about any openings there.

✓ Maintain regular contact with your interviewer. Every month send him or her a fax, call on the phone, arrange another meeting, or drop by for a visit. Update him or her on your search, especially if you receive or think you'll receive another offer.

✓ Even if you get another job, keep the communication lines open. Send a fax on your new company stationery informing your interviewer of your new position. You may become a more desirable candidate, as some people do when hired by another company.

15
Stepping Back, Moving Forward

Introduction

Are you still stuck or struggling with your job search? Perhaps you've completed most or all of the exercises in this book but you still don't seem any closer to a job than you were before you started "exercising." Or it could be that these activities have helped you a great deal in your search—you are now going on interviews for jobs that really seem right for you—but you still don't have an offer. Or maybe you're receiving offers for jobs you don't want.

No matter which of these descriptions applies to you, something is probably wrong with your approach to the search process. The purpose of this chapter is to identify the flaw and correct it.

We're strong believers in process improvement. Over the years we've helped thousands of individuals and organizations achieve higher levels of teamwork, resolve conflicts, and reach other goals through process improvement. In all these instances, the key to improvement was stepping back and evaluating the process. With hindsight, it's often easy to see where a mistake was made or a barrier erected. You might find, for instance, that you unconsciously erected a barrier to any job that required public speaking. Or you might discover that you never identified a certain skill you possess. Once you identify where your job search process went off course, you can get it back on track.

The activities in this chapter will help you do so, using the four-step model on the following page.

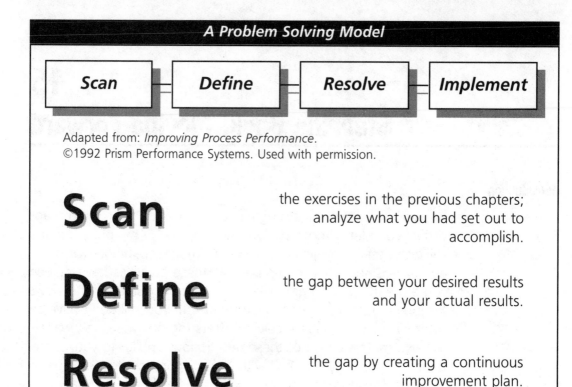

Scan
the exercises in the previous chapters; analyze what you had set out to accomplish.

Define
the gap between your desired results and your actual results.

Resolve
the gap by creating a continuous improvement plan.

Implement
your plan, anticipate potential barriers, and plan to resolve or manage them.

91. SCAN

The diagram on the following page provides you with a summary of activity categories from previous chapters. We'd like you to review each category—or what we're referring to here as a process step—and determine how well you did with each one. After you've evaluated the eight steps listed in the table that follows the diagram, you should note the specific actions needed to improve the way you deal with a given part of the process.

Strategic Career Search Model & Outline

Defining Yourself

Identify Values Interests Emotions

Determine Skill Package

Ch. 1 & 2

Ch. 3 & 4

Targeting Your Market

List Potential Jobs

Identify Valued Organizations

Search for Potential Organizations

Choose Targeted Employers

Ch. 5

Ch. 6

Ch. 7

Ch. 8

Securing Your Position

Networking

Interviewing

Rating Performance

Managing the Offers

Reviewing the Process

Preparing Next Steps

Ch. 9 & 10

Ch. 11 & 12

Ch. 13

Ch. 14

Ch. 15

Ch. 16

101 Tools Section Step	Completed?	Target #	Actual # Improvement	Continuous
Identified Values, Interests, & Emotions?	YES/NO	N/A	N/A	
Identified Skill Package?	YES/NO	N/A	N/A	
Identified Potential Jobs?	YES/NO	15		
Identified Potential Organizations?	YES/NO	100		
Identified Valued Organizations?	YES/NO	25		
Identified Target Organizations?	YES/NO	15		
Interviewed for Positions?	YES/NO	10		
Received Offers for Review?	YES/NO	3		

92. 20-20 HINDSIGHT

As useful as the first part of this exercise is, it doesn't give you the whole story. It's important to add a more subjective perspective to your evaluation. You may have a better sense about how well (or poorly) you did with a step of the process than the table allows you to demonstrate. For that reason, we'd like you to consider the following questions:

1. The responses you gave around your values, interests, emotions: Looking back, would you change anything? If yes, what changes would you make?
2. The responses you gave for your skill package: How well do they match with the potential jobs you identified? Do you need to go back and identify some additional jobs that more closely or broadly match your skills? What would you change?
3. The potential, valued, and targeted organizations/employers you identified: Are they the right type? How closely do they match your skills and values? How easily were you able to identify each kind of organization? Do you need to expand your search or add different kinds of organizations? What would you add?
4. The results of your interviews and offers: Review your interview practice sheets and evaluations. What areas can you improve on? What kind of feedback did you get from interviewers? What can you do to improve?

93. DEFINE

When we say define, we mean we'd like you to specify what went well and what went wrong as you worked through the exercises. Think about it in terms of the gap between what you set out to do and what you actually accomplished. It is easiest if you can define the gap in terms of several bullet points such as:

✓ didn't clearly define my skill set
✓ failed to identify enough potential organizations
✓ settled for interviews outside of my valued organization list

In the space below, define the gap as best you can:

■
■
■
■
■
■
■
■

Now list where gaps don't exist, where you accomplished what you set out to do. Again, put this in the form of bulleted points:

-
-
-
-
-
-
-
-

If you're having trouble with this exercise, talk about it with someone—a friend or a mentor, perhaps. We've found that dialogue about defining issues helps to clarify them.

94. RESOLVE

In the previous exercise, you identified gaps between what you set out to accomplish and what you achieved in your career search activities. Now, think about ways you can close those gaps—what can you do to identify your skills, to do better at interviews, to improve the way in which you telemarket yourself? What we're asking you to do here is create an action plan, a plan stated in terms of:

✓ the positive
✓ specific steps
✓ measurable actions
✓ achievable outcomes
✓ realistic goals
✓ timely activities

In the space below, develop your continuous improvement action plan for resolving the gap.

Gap	Skill Needed	Action(s) to Be Taken	Ways to Measure Progress

95. IMPLEMENT

Easier said than done, right? Implementing your plan from the previous exercise is what we're asking you to do, but you may find it difficult to put it into action. Based on our experience with action planning, barriers frequently arise that stop plans in their tracks. To overcome those barriers, it's best to think about them in advance. Specifically, what obstacles do you anticipate preventing you from carrying out your plan?

It may be that you want to follow our networking exercises but you anticipate falling back on the same old list of contacts to help you get a job. Or you might recognize that you're too shy in interviews to articulate your strengths in a positive, impactful manner. These are barriers that can be overcome if they're identified and analyzed.

Barrier busting refers to the element of action planning that recognizes that there are bound to be challenges or barriers to any plan, and it's best to identify these potential barriers as soon as possible in the process. There are actually two aspects to barrier busting.

The first aspect is the proactive identification of potential barriers. Identifying barriers as you create your plan can help keep you from being hit by surprises that can set your search process back a few steps or more.

The second aspect is the analysis of the barriers, challenging your own thinking about the barriers and what can be done to overcome them. Sometimes the barriers we identify are real and can be overwhelming. At times though, the real barrier is in our thinking. Many times, the barriers fall somewhere in between. We believe it is important to understand the difference so you can create an effective plan to manage or remove the barriers that keep you from being successful in your career search. The three types of barriers are described on the next page.

Barrier Busting

Barriers can fall into one of three major categories …

It appears impossible to take action—people, policies, or other factors are preventing you.

Ask yourself:
✓ Can I remove it or change it?
✓ Can I get around it?
✓ Is there another way?

Action is possible, but you feel limited in how much you can accomplish without additional support/resources.

Ask yourself:
✓ Can I get someone to help me?
✓ Can I modify my plan in some way?
✓ Will it help if I let go of some things?

We all know what these are—barriers brought about by our own thinking patterns, habits, and level of comfort.

Ask yourself:
✓ What's the worst that could happen?
✓ What if I don't take action?
✓ What's the risk in doing nothing?

Adapted from: *Positive Leadership.*
© 1992. Prism Performance Systems. Used with permission.

Examine your plan. Review the barriers you identified. As you list each of your barriers on this page, ask yourself if it's a **BLOCK**, a **LIMIT,** or an **ILLUSION.**

Once you have identified the type of barrier you are facing, create actions to either remove or manage the barrier.

Barrier	Type	Action	By When	Resources

16

Your Career Search Doesn't End with Your Next Job

Introduction

Unlike books, career searches seldom have last chapters anymore. Much of what our parents and grandparents believed about the world of work has become mere myths. With rare exceptions, you are unlikely to find:

✓ the 40-hour workweek
✓ employment for life/job security
✓ the gold watch for 25 years of service
✓ retirement at age 65
✓ performing a single job function in your organization
✓ long-established work processes
✓ total reliance on the past to predict the future
✓ top-down decision making
✓ creating/finding your niche
✓ reaching a goal and relaxing

Instead, if our experiences hold true, you are likely to see:

✓ increasing reliance on teams to make decisions
✓ constant challenging of the status quo
✓ an expectation that people become "multiple threat players"
✓ a continued movement toward organizational learning
✓ a realization that customers are both internal and external
✓ constant innovation and experimentation
✓ challenging of long-held paradigms

To survive in the twenty-first century, organizations are going to have to be able to satisfy customers in ways seldom imagined in earlier times. Today's customers are continually pushing their requirements higher—higher quality, more reliable delivery, and all at lower prices. As a result, organizations and their employees have had to learn how to learn, change, and adapt at an ever-increasing pace.

Over the last several years, our organization, Prism Performance Systems, has worked with everyone from small, family-owned companies to huge, Fortune 100 firms, helping them with the human side of performance improvement and change. During that time, we've observed certain trends that impact career and job performance. For instance, employers have begun to expect that employees will develop certain skills beyond those of their traditional job descriptions. Some of those, like computer skills and working in teams, are widely known and accepted. Others include such things as the ability to cope with change, tolerate ambiguity, resolve conflict, and manage stress.

Do you possess these skills? The next exercise gives you the opportunity to find out.

96. ARE YOU A NEW OR OLD PARADIGM TYPE OF PERSON?

1. **When a major change occurs at work, I usually try to ...**

   _____ **a.** look on the bright side and see what I can do to help.

   _____ **b.** look for how the change will hurt me personally.

   _____ **c.** look for a way out—figuring I had better start circulating my resume soon.

   _____ **d.** ignore it and hope it will go away—change seldom lasts anyway.

   _____ **e.** approach it as a challenge that I can help lead.

2. **When it comes to making decisions and taking action I ...**

   _____ **a.** like to have a clear and specific plan to follow.

   _____ **b.** could never rely on someone who can't support their position with sufficient facts and data.

   _____ **c.** expect my managers and their managers to have all the plans worked out first.

   _____ **d.** recognize that life is too complicated for easy "yes" or "no" answers.

   _____ **e.** take things as they happen, without worrying too much about it in advance.

3. **When handling conflict on the job, I most often try to ...**

   _____ **a.** find a compromise solution.

   _____ **b.** sacrifice my own needs for the needs of the other person.

   _____ **c.** win my position in order to get my own way.

   _____ **d.** be fair and work to see that both our needs are met.

   _____ **e.** postpone the issue or avoid taking a position until I can think it over or it goes away.

4. When stress in the workplace begins to build up, I ...

_____ **a.** look for a way to avoid it personally affecting me.

_____ **b.** become more focused in my work and duties and try not to let it get to me.

_____ **c.** find that I get more edgy and argumentative.

_____ **d.** talk things out and see how I can adapt.

_____ **e.** go home and kick the dog.

If you answered either "a" or "e" to question 1, it may suggest that you see change as an opportunity. Answering either "b," "c," or "d" might suggest that you see change as more of a danger.

Answering either "a," "b," or "c" to question 2 implies that you have a low tolerance for ambiguity, while answering either "d" or "e" could mean that you are more comfortable when you can operate more flexibly, without being tied to deadlines and objectives.

Answering "a" to question 3 indicates that you are a compromiser. Answering" b" might suggest you are more of an accommodator when it comes to managing conflict. Answering "c" could mean you are a competitive conflict handler, while an answer of "e" types you as an avoider. An answer of "d" could indicate you prefer to collaborate when resolving conflict, a trait that is becoming more and more sought after at work.

For question 4, an answer of "a" may indicate your way of handling stress is what is referred to as _flight._ An answer of "b" leads us to conclude that your method is to _freeze._ Answering "c" could suggest that when it comes to stress you use a _fight_ response; and answering "d" could indicate that you seek to relieve stress by exploring it or talking it out. Answering "e" could indicate that you have a hard time managing stress.

There are no right or wrong answers to these four questions, so don't give yourself a failing or passing grade. Instead, look at your responses in a more holistic sense. Do they reveal a person who is adept at coping with new workplace trends or one who seems more comfortable in an environment that's quickly disappearing?

97. ACQUIRING SKILLS

Perhaps the most harmful work myth is that employers will be responsible for your professional growth and development. The objective of most organizations' training programs is getting their people up to speed. To acquire the new skills that will keep or make you marketable, you're on your own (though some organizations will continue to pay for seminars and schooling).

This exercise will help you begin that process. We've provided you with a worksheet that lists a series of questions related to skill acquisition and provides some sample answers. Complete the worksheet as it applies to your future career goals. If you're having problems completing it, talk to your supervisor or, if you're out of work, a career coach or someone in your industry who you respect. They'll be able to give you a sense of what skills will be marketable in the future.

Targeting My Future Goals

Answer the questions below as they relate to you personally and professionally.

What else would you like to do?

Example: (On the job) Work with creative people.
             (Off the job) Hunt and fish; this requires patience, perseverance, and precision.

What can that translate to on your job?

Example: Seek out opportunities to work on teams and small groups that are assigned specific, detailed tasks to accomplish (like coming up with a new order form for computer services).

Who do you know doing that?

Example: Assistant Project Manager for Quality Improvement.

Answer the questions below as they relate to you personally and professionally.

What characteristics does that person have that you would like to have?

Example: He/she has latitude to recommend/select different people to work on teams. He/she selects tasks to be studied that are precise, easy to see, and usually doable.

In what professional skill areas are you strongest?

Example: Getting along with people, detailing tasks, seeing tasks to the end, helping people see the "how to" in completing a task.

How can you use them to build additional skills?

Example: These are the basics for team leader development, as well as effective supervision.

In what professional areas do you need the greatest improvement?

Example: Experience with delegation; working in small groups on jobs not in my areas of specialty (i.e., personnel recruiting); role of supervisor, giving recognition and improvement feedback.

What can you do to improve them?

Example: a. Let my supervisor know of my job needs and wants.

              b. Openly volunteer for assignments to small teams and ask for task team authority.

What is a reasonable short-term (6-24 months) development goal for you?

Example: Assistant Project Manager for a team.

If you are not sure where your interests and skills or talents would be best used in your organization, with whom can you talk to find out?

98. WHAT YOU DON'T KNOW ABOUT YOUR TARGETED SKILLS CAN HURT YOU

If only skills could be purchased at some multi-skill superstore! It would certainly be a lot easier than the uncertain process most people go through as they attempt to develop expertise in a key area.

Still, it isn't as if you're the first one ever to attempt to acquire a given skill. There are plenty of other people who have blazed skill-acquisition trails, and it makes sense to follow in their footsteps.

The following activity will guide you through an interview with a person who has developed the skills you want.

Developmental Information Interview Guide

You are to interview someone who holds a job/position you would like to consider for your future. This could be someone in an advanced position within your current career, or someone with an entirely different career you would consider. You want to gather as much information as possible to complete an Individual Development Plan (Exercise 99).

1. Identify the position this individual currently holds.

2. Identify the developmental track (skill level) that led him/her to his/her current position.

3. For the purpose of learning as much as you can about the new skills, gather the following information:
   a. What are the primary task responsibilities?

   b. What skills are needed to carry out each responsibility?

   c. How long has this person been doing the task?

   d. How did he/she learn the task?

   e. What did he/she do before? And before that? And before that? What steps led to the current skill level? What other steps could lead to it?

   f. Does this person like what he/she is doing now? (What are the greatest benefits of their job functions? What are the biggest drawbacks?)

   g. What would this person do differently if he/she had the chance to do it again?

   h. What advice could he/she give you about preparing for a skill level like this?

4. Ask other questions to gather as much information as you can. Take good notes. You may use this information in a real coaching session with your manager.

99. INDIVIDUAL DEVELOPMENT PLANNING

It's time to make another plan. The following charts will help you (1) determine your skill objectives; (2) figure out actions to meet those objectives; and (3) identify the level of skill desired.

Individual Development Plan

Employee Name (Last, First, Middle Initial)	
Current Job Title:	Unit:

Skill Development Objective	Targeted Skill Development
	Short-Term (next 12 months)

Strengths: (Summarize particularly strong skills and behaviors displayed on the job, and strengths to target for greater utilization.)

Current Strengths	Needed/Required for Targeted Skills/Tasks

Development Needs: (Below, indicate skills which need to be developed, or knowledge to be gained.)

Current Position	Needed/Required for Targeted Skills/Tasks

100. GIVING BACK

Return back to the very first chapters in which you identified your current skill sets. Combine these with the developmental skills you identified earlier in this chapter. Create a list of the skills you wish to contribute to your organization. As you list your skills, indicate whether your contribution now and in the future will be as a:

✓ learner - apprentice
✓ worker - craftsperson
✓ coach - master builder

■
■
■
■
■
■
■
■

101. WORK YOUR WAY TO THE TOP

It's impossible to predict where your career will take you, but it helps to visualize the most positive direction possible. By keeping an ideal career track in your head (and on paper), you have a guide to your ultimate job. This final five-step exercise is designed to do exactly that.

1. Write a description of the ultimate job to which you aspire. Include the job title (CEO, partner, bank president, etc.) Be as specific as possible in describing the position, including the type of organization you'd like to work for in that position (Fortune 100 company, top ten accounting firm), as well as the job responsibilities.

2. Write a description of the job that would lead to this ultimate job. In other words, what position would be a stepping stone to the ultimate one. Again, be specific in terms of titles and responsibilities.

3. Write a description of one or two other jobs that would lead to the position you described in step 2, including titles and responsibilities.

4. Given the positions you've identified in the previous three steps, what would be the single biggest obstacle that would prevent you from obtaining these positions? After writing down the obstacle, create some ideas for overcoming it. For instance, perhaps you feel the major obstacle is learning how to play politics. One way to overcome that obstacle would be to align yourself with a powerful mentor; another would be to work with a career coach who can teach you some political skills.

5. Given the positions described, what attribute or skill that you possess makes it possible that you can achieve your ultimate job? Simply write a sentence or two explaining how that attribute or skill might power you along your career path.

Just because you've come to the end of the book doesn't mean you should stop exercising. You certainly can and should revisit the 101 activities; you may find that the way you answer questions, fill in blanks, and solve problems will change at different points in your career. In fact, the difference in how you respond at Point A in your career, versus, Point B might be a great learning experience.

At the very least, we hope you'll keep returning to Chapter 15. The career planning activities there are designed to be used many times. By necessity, your career goals will change as you gain new experience and expertise. Continuous improvement of your plan will increase the odds that you'll meet your new goals.

Some of you may already have used this book's exercises to obtain new jobs or embark on new career paths. Others may still be trying to find their way. Whatever your situation, we hope all of you will keep relying on what you've learned from the book and apply it.

Above all else, don't give up. Let the process work for you. Each of the authors can cite personal experiences with changing careers and overcoming challenges associated with finding a new job or creating one. Unfortunately, none of us had this book to help us when we were going through the process. We did, however, use informal versions of the exercises, quizzes, and other activities in this book. By formalizing them, we hope to make the process easier for you. Forget the old strategies and old rules, and start fresh. Power up your search with the catalysts and guides in these pages.

We'd like to hear about your experiences. You are our experts. You will no doubt discover other alternatives for conducting a career search. You will also discover your own methods and activities that serve you well. As big believers in networking and continuously learning, we would love to share them with others and incorporate them in our next book. You can reach us at:

Prism Performance Systems, Inc.
37000 Grand River, Suite 230
Farmington Hills, Michigan 48335
810-474-8855
FAX: 810-474-1116
www.PrismPerformance.com

Index

Achievement, as career guide, 5
Accomplishments:
  leveraging, 23-34
  My Greatest Accomplishments worksheet, 32
  turning into skills, 33-34
  writing your greatest, 31-32
Acquiring Skills (97), 211-212
Activate Your Pitch (69), 147
Alien Encounter (17), 29
Amiables (work style), 43, 44, 47
Analyticals (work style), 44, 47
Anger and blame, in spiral of descending emotions, 9
Are These Organizations Right for You? (43), 96
  Targeting Organizations Matrix, 96
Are You a New or Old Paradigm Type of Person? (96), 209-210
Attributes, as aspect of skills, 37-39
  Attributes Worksheet, 38-39
Attributes: A to Z (21), 37

Back to the Want Ads (37), 78
Banking, financial type of organization, 136
Barrier busting, 204-206
Brainstorming Information Sources (38), 79-81

Career help, xiii-xiv
Choose Your Ideal Working Environment (10), 18
Choose Your Organizational Culture (12), 20
Choose Your Power Words (25), 49-51
Cold calling for interviews, 145-146
Comfort zone:
  finding, 21-22
  types of, 20
Continuous improvement plan, 203
Creating Your Own Rumor (58), 127
Cut Through the Clutter (65), 138

Define (93), 201-202

Defining yourself, 3-11
Denial, in spiral of descending emotions, 9
Developmental Information Interview Guide, 214
Development planning, individual, 215
Draw Your Own Conclusions (33), 70-71
  Job Characteristics Survey—Part 1, 71
Dream jobs, and reality, 65-66
Drivers (work style), 43, 44, 47

Emotions, in a job search, 7-8
Employers:
  evaluating, 77-94
  finding out about, 95-105
  knowing, 174-175
Enjoyment, as career guide, 5
Excitement and hope, in spiral of descending emotions, 9
Experiences, learning from, 28
Expertise, as career guide, 5
Expressives (work style), 44, 47
Express Yourself (4), 9
Extra Credit Questions (75), 160-161

Family, as career guide, 5
Favorable Odds (68), 145-146
Fear and dread, in spiral of descending emotions, 9, 10
Feelings, as career guide, 3-11
Finding Information Nuggets (47), 101-104
Finding Your Comfort Zone (13), 21
Find the Shared Trait (55), 122-123
Find the Strengths in Your Style (23), 45-46
Find Your Sticking Points (5), 10
Friendship, as career guide, 5
From Fantasy to Reality (30), 65
Fun Things to Do with Resumes (61), 131-132

Getting the Word Out (59), 128
Getting Unstuck (6), 11

Giving Back (100), 216
Goals, targeting, 211-210
Gossip, as souce of information, 107-108
Grade Your Resume (60), 130

Helplessness, in spiral of descending emotions, 9, 10
High technology type of organization, 136
Hindsight, use of, in job search, 200
Hopelessness, in spiral of descending emotions, 9, 10
Human services type of organization, 136

If All Else Fails—Last Resort Tactics (71), 150-151
If You Still Can't Decide (88), 192
Implement (95), 204-206
Independence, as career guide, 5
Individual Development Planning (99), 215
Industrial Espionage (42), 93-94
Industry knowledge, use of, 89-92
Inside information, on organizations, 109-110
Inside Stuff (50), 109-110
Instant Replay: Keeping a What/How "Tape" of the Action (78), 166
Interviewer:
    knowing, 156-159
    role of, 137
Interviewing with Style (76), 162
Interview Report Card, The (82), 176
Interviews:
    cold calling for, 142-143, 145-146
    communicating in, 26-27, 29-30
    evaluating, 165-181
    frequently asked questions, 153-155, 160-161
    how to request, 148
    losing resolve, 111
    phases of, 166-169
    preparing answers for, 173
    preparing for, 105-111, 149-165
    report card for, 176
    Request for Job Interview Checklist, 148
    researching organizations before, 101-104
    self-analysis in, 170-172
    what to do after, 184-185
    wrong answers, 177-181
Involve-oriented organization, 20
I Will Not Be Tempted by ... (51), 111

Job:
    characteristics, 70-71
        Job Characteristics Survey—Part 1, 71
    choosing, 59-76
    criteria, 60-62, 63-64
    dream, 65-66
    and likes/dislikes, 72-73
    matching types of, with organizations, 82-85, 86-88
    myths about, 207-208
    writing descriptions of, 217
Job search, last resort tactics, 150-151

Knowing Your Interviewer (74), 156-159
Knowing yourself, 35-56
Knowledge Is Power (77), 163-164
Know Thy Employer (81), 174-175

Life events, significance in the interview, 26-27
Lifeline (14), 24-25
Likes/dislikes, and job selection, 72-73
Listening to the Gossip (49), 107-108
Location, as career guide, 5
Look for Your Blind Spot (7), 11
Loyalty, as career guide, 5

Magic Formula (85), 186-189
Magnet Skill (32), 69
Making the Grade on the Job (72), 152
    Making the Grade on the Job worksheet, 152
Manufacturing type of organization, 136
Match Game, The (35), 74-75
Misrepresentation, consequences of, 142-143
Mix Your Networks (56), 124
Multiple Choice—Test What's Really Important to You (28), 60-62
Multiply the Possibilities (40), 86-88

Negotiating the Numbers (87), 191
Negotiating the offer, 190
Network, building, 115-128
    communicating within, 128
    identifying shared traits in, 122-123
    identifying yours, 119
    mixing, 124
    rumors, use of in, 127
    targeting, 120-121
        shifting targets within, 125-126

Networking Instinct Quotient (NIQ) (52), 116-118

Objections, overcoming, 144
Observations of you, by others, 52-54
Offer:
   deciding on, 192
   evaluating, 186-187
   negotiating, 191
   questions to ask before accepting, 190
   responding to, 183-196
Organization/Job Type Matching (39), 82-85
Organizations:
   gossip about, 107-108
   identifying the worst/best, 99-100
   inside information on, 109-110
   matching with job types, 82-85, 86-88
   researching, 97-98, 101-104, 163-164
   selection of, on basis of industry knowledge, 89-92
   Targeting Organizations Matrix, 96, 187-188
   types of, 136

Paradigms, 209-210
Perfect Comeback Line, The (67), 144
Personal depreciation, in spiral of descending emotions, 9, 10
Phone Dialogue Quotient (66), 142
Post-Interview Puzzlers (84), 184-185
Power, as career guide, 5
Power words, choosing, 49-51
Preferences:
   matching with job, 74-75
   summarizing, 76
Problem Solving Model, 198
Putting Your Best Piece of Paper Forward—Role of Interviewer (64), 137
Putting Your Best Piece of Paper Forward—Type of Organization (63), 136

Quick Quiz—The Weirdest Job Interview You'll Never Have (15), 26-27

Reality Check (2), 4-6
Rebounding from Rejection (89), 193-194
Refining Your Choices (34), 72-73
Rejection:
   rebounding from, 193-194
   turning into acceptance, 195

Research, on organizations, 97-98
Resolve (94), 203
Resumes, 129-140
   characteristics of, 130
   fun with, 131
   unusual types, 138-139
   using more than one, 133-135
Rumors, use of, in networking, 127

Sadness, in spiral of descending emotions, 9, 10
Sales type of organization, 136
SCAN (91), 198-199
Scavenger Hunt (44), 97-98
Security, as career guide, 5
Seeing Yourself Through Others' Eyes (26), 52-54
Self-Analysis (79), 170-172
Self-realization, as career guide, 5
Selling yourself, 35-56
Service, as career guide, 5
Seven Questions to Ask Before Accepting Any Offer (86), 190
Shock/rejection/frustration, in spiral of descending emotions, 9, 10
Significant Experiences (16), 28
Skill Comparison Analysis (48), 106
Skills:
   acquiring, 211-212
   comparing, 106
   contributing to the organization, 216
   derived from accomplishments, 33-34
   magnet, 69
   matching with job, 74-75
   selection of, 36
   summarizing, 76
   in terms of attributes, 37-39
   use of:
      in employee selection, 79
      in job selection, 55
   what you don't know about, 213-214
      Developmental Information Interview Guide, 214
Skill Selecting (20), 36
So You Wanna Be a ... (27), 55-56
Spiral of Descending Emotions (3), 7-8
   and blind spots, 11
   breaking, 11

State Your Preferences (9), 16
Strategic Career Search Model & Outline, iv, xi, 199
Styles:
    finding strengths of, 45-46
    in interviewing, 162
    translating into work behaviors, 47-48
    of working, 40-44

12 Things to Do When You're Asking for an Interview (70), 148
    Request for Job Interview Checklist, 148
20-20 Hindsight (92), 200
25 Questions Interviewers Frequently Ask (73), 153-155
Targeting My Future Goals worksheet, 211-212
Targeting Organizations Matrix, 187-188
Target Shifting (57), 125-176
Team-oriented organization, 20
Telemarketing, in a job search, 141-148
Tell-oriented organizaton, 20
Ten Best List, The (46), 100
Ten Worst List, The (45), 99
Things to Do with My Accomplishments (18), 31-32
    My Greatest Accomplishments worksheet, 32
Traits, evaluation of, 152
Translating Your Style into Work Behaviors (24), 47-48
Traps, 13-22
    Job-Finding Traps worksheet, 15

Try to Find Your Personal Caereer Trap (8), 14
Turn Back the Clock (80), 173
Turning Accomplishments into Skills (19), 33-34
Two Resumes for the Price of One (62), 133
    resume worksheets, 134-135

Values, as career guide, 3-11
    Worksheet (2), 5

Want ads, use of, in evaluating employers, 78
Wanted: The Perfect Job (29), 63-64
Wealth, as career guide, 5
What's Wrong with This Interview? (83), 177-181
What You Don't Know about Your Targeted Skills Can Hurt You (98), 213-214
Where Do I Need Career Help? (1), xiii-xiv
Wishes, 16
Word Association (11), 19-20
Work criteria, 16-17
    Work Criteria Preferences worksheet, 17
Work environment:
    choosing, 18
    worst-case, 67-68
Working with Style: Which One Fits You? (22), 40-44
Work Your Way to the Top (101), 217
Worst-Case Scenarios (31), 67-68

Your Surprise Package (36), 76

About the Authors

The authors are all associated with Prism Performance Systems, a Detroit-area change management consulting firm that works with some of the world's leading corporations on career, team-building, training, and other change-related issues. Their clients include Rubbermaid, Cadillac, Hanna Barbera, Chevrolet, IBM, and the Lazy Boy Chair Company. Their expertise is in designing processes, simulations, games, and a wide variety of tools to facilitate individual and organizational objectives. Tom Buck is Prism's president and speaks and writes frequently on change management subjects. Bill Matthews has taught college courses in educational games and simulations and is a senior consultant at Prism. Bob Leech works closely with Prism on numerous projects through his consulting firm, R.N. Leech & Associates, and has extensive experience in career counseling.